Fly-Fishing Tales of T

Fly-Fishing Tales of Terror

by Bob Zahn

Menasha Ridge Press
Birmingham, Alabama

Copyright © 1999 by Bob Zahn
All rights reserved
Printed in the United States of America
Published by Menasha Ridge Press
First edition, first printing

Library of Congress Cataloging-in-Publication Data

Zahn, Bob, 1934—
    Fly-fishing tales of terror / Bob Zahn.
        p. cm.
    ISBN 0-89732-278-9
    1. Fly-fishing—Caricatures and cartoons. 2. American wit and humor, Pictorial. I. Title.
NC1429.Z24A4 1998
741.5'973—dc21   98-37690
                        CIP

Menasha Ridge Press
P. O. Box 43059
Birmingham, AL 35243
(800) 247-9437
www.menasharidge.com

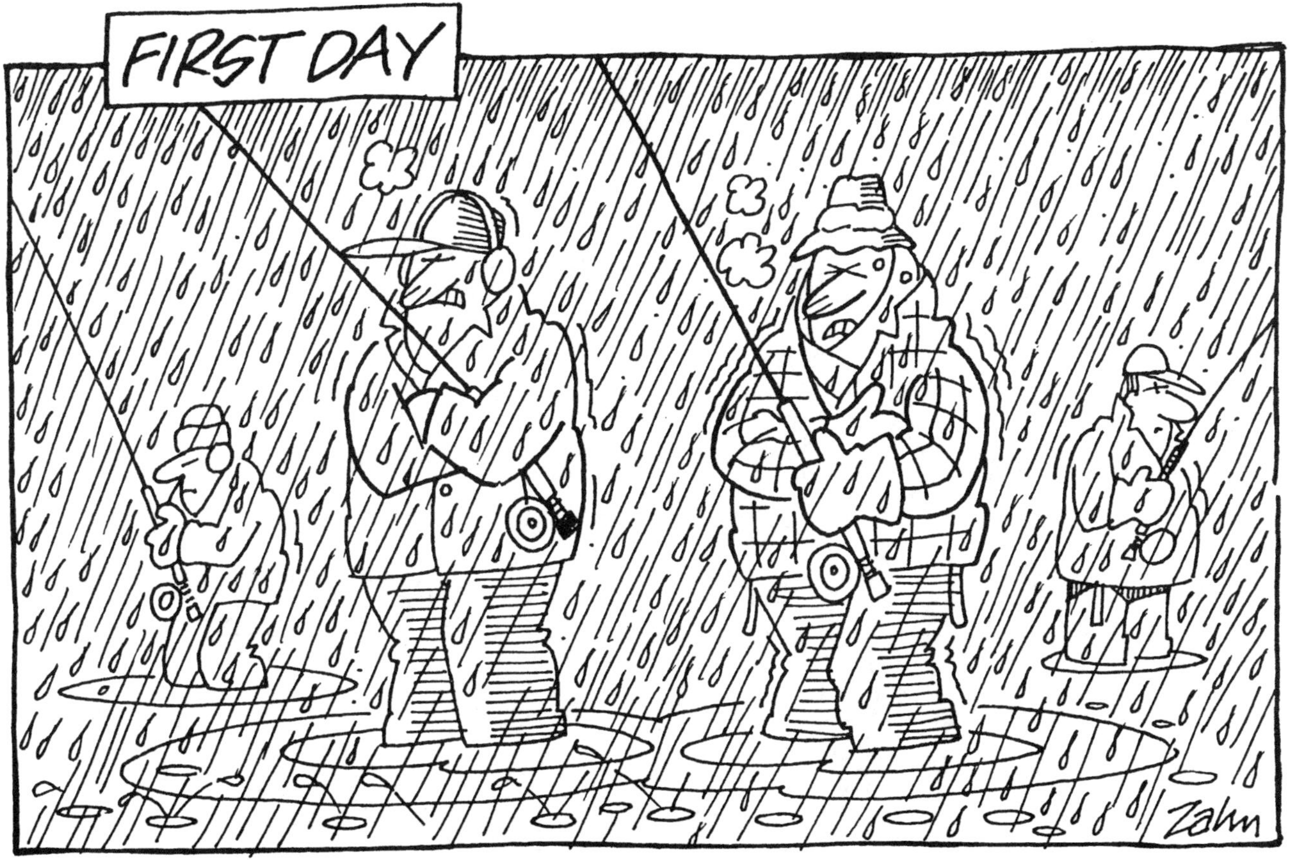
FIRST DAY
Zahn

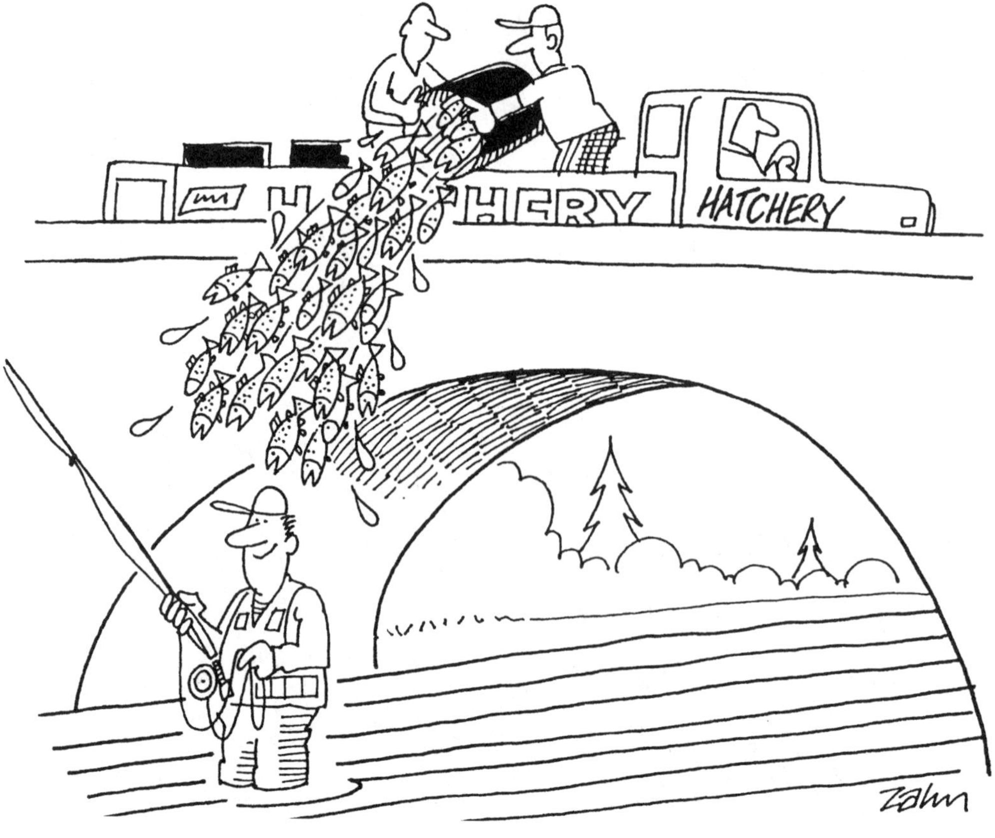
HATCHERY
zahn

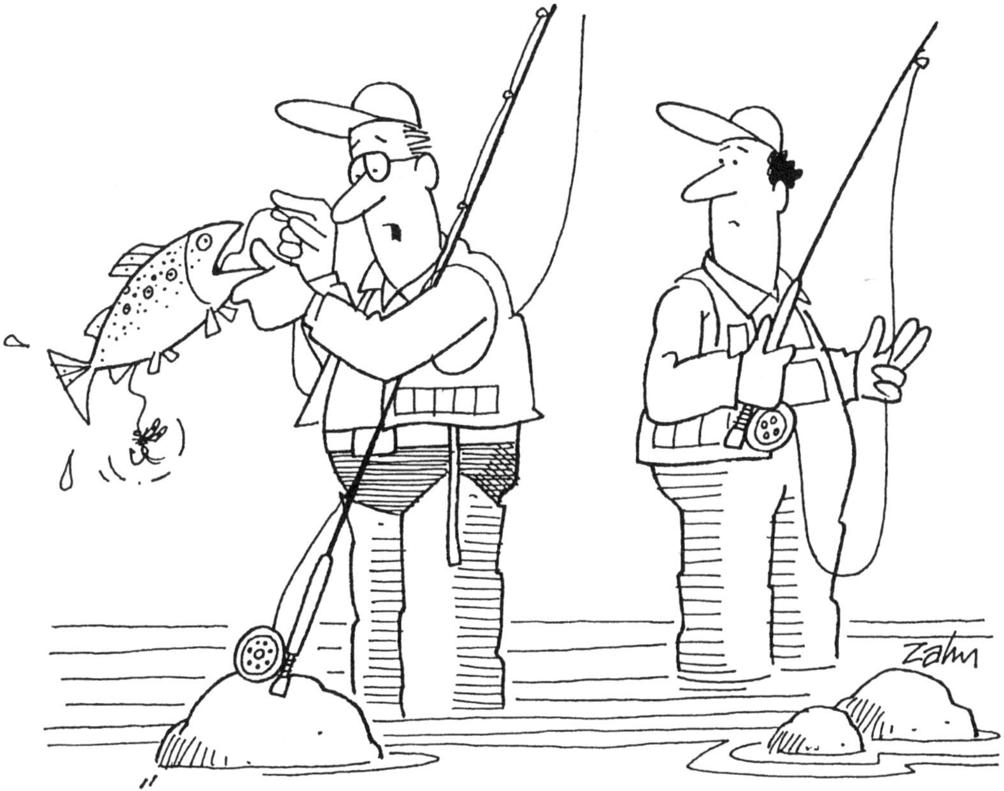
zahn

"OH, OH! HE SWALLOWED IT!"

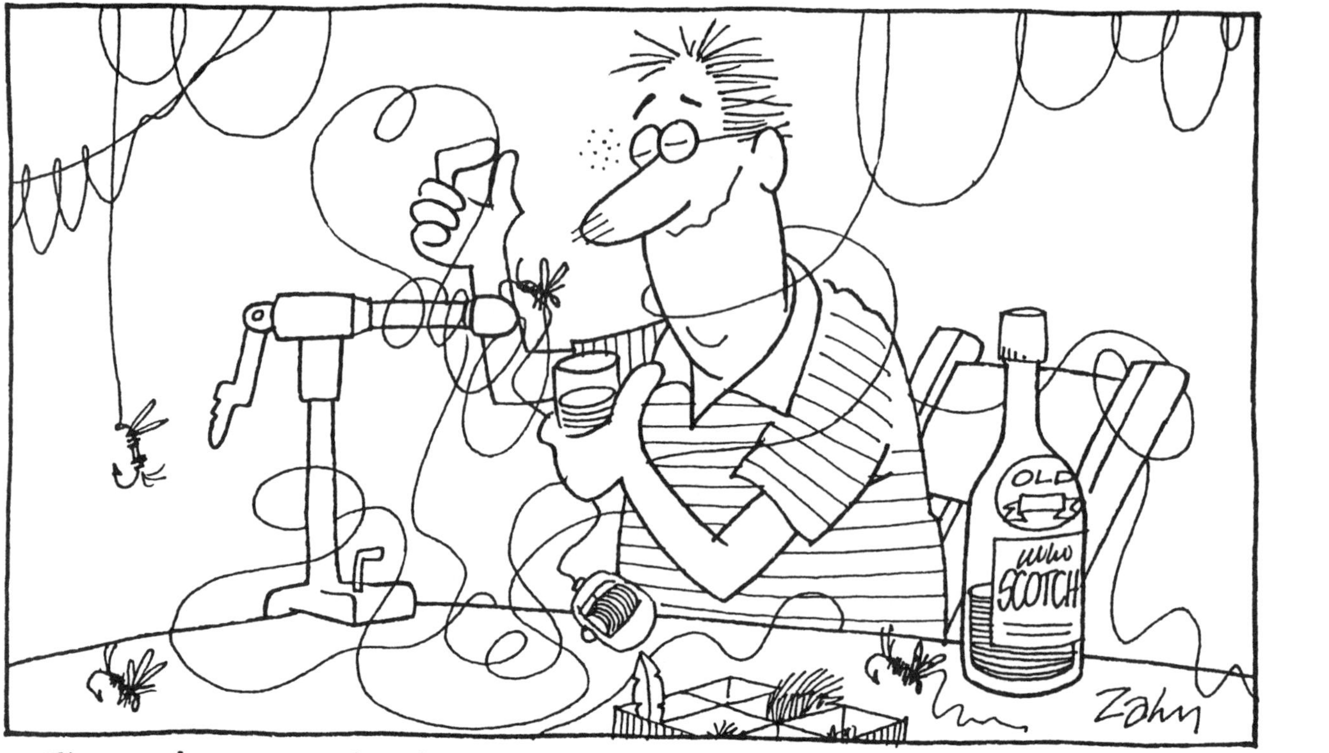
OLD
SCOTCH
Zahn

Floyd was tying more than one on...

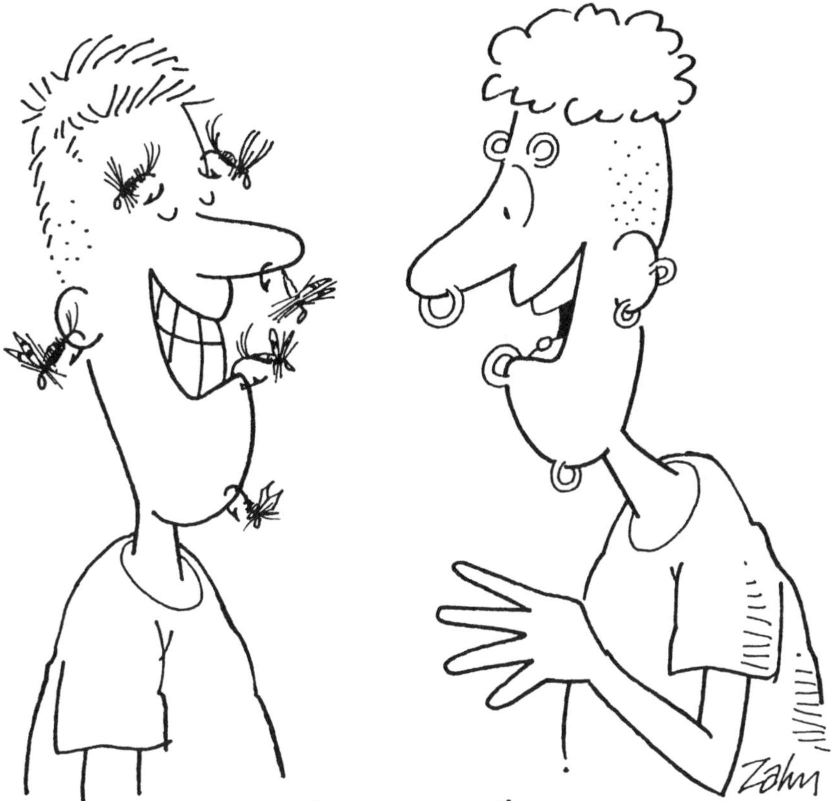
Zahn

"COOL!"

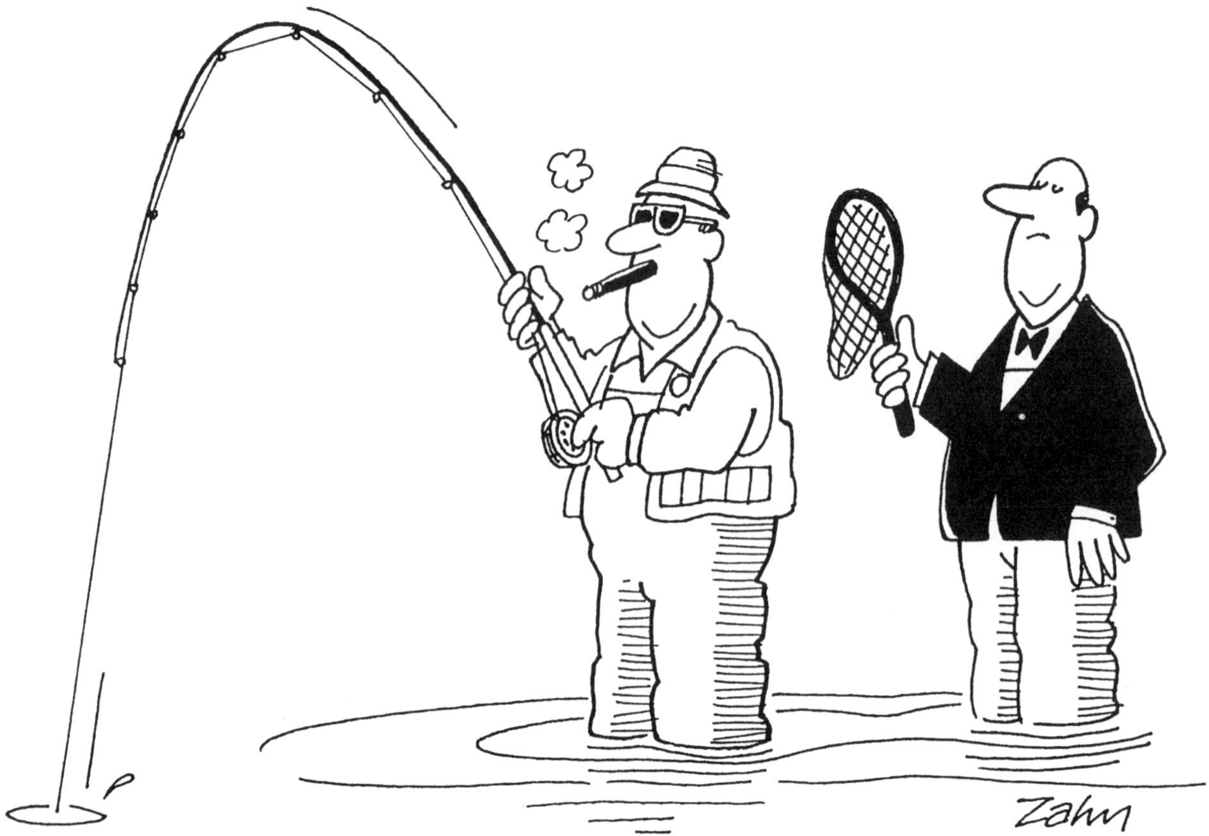
Zahn

Adams

"Grizzly" Adams

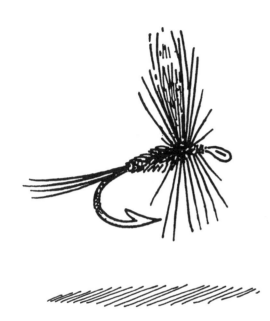

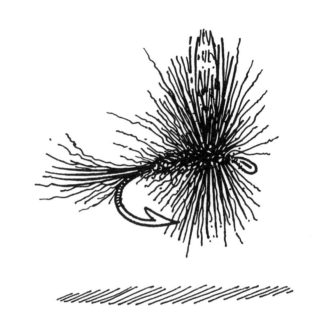

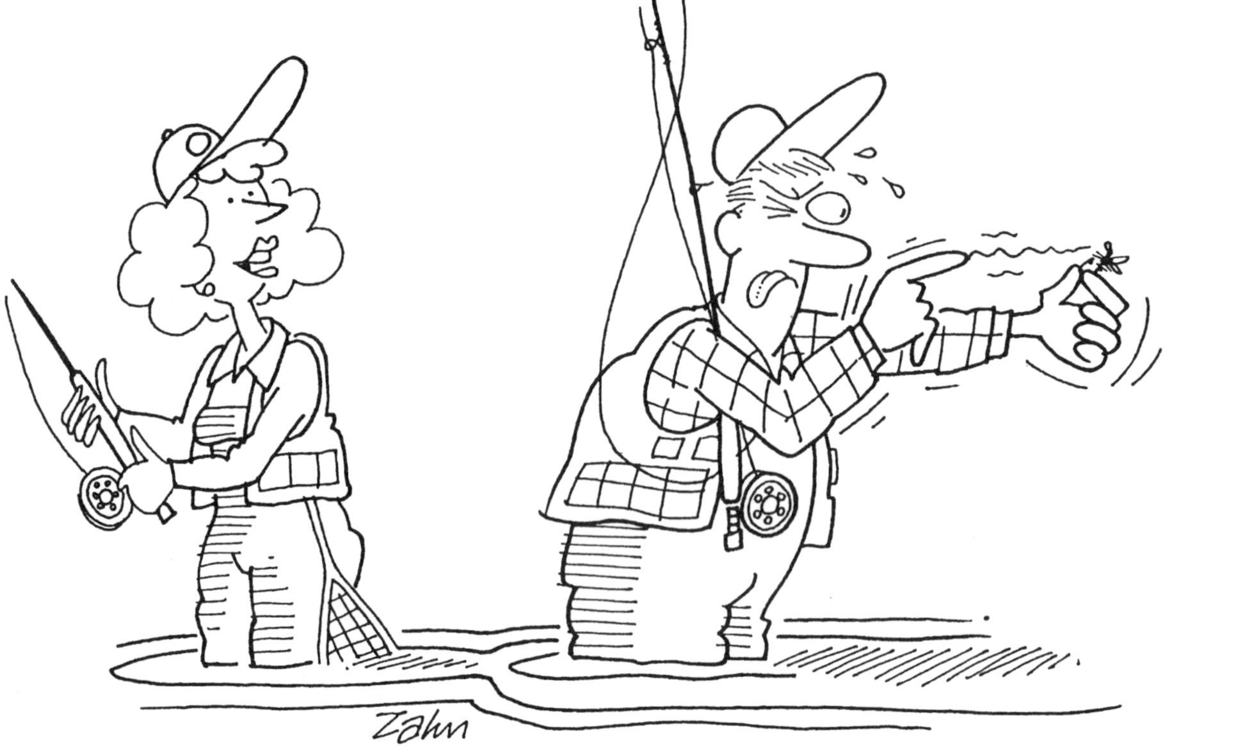
Zahn

"YOU FORGOT YOUR GLASSES AGAIN?"

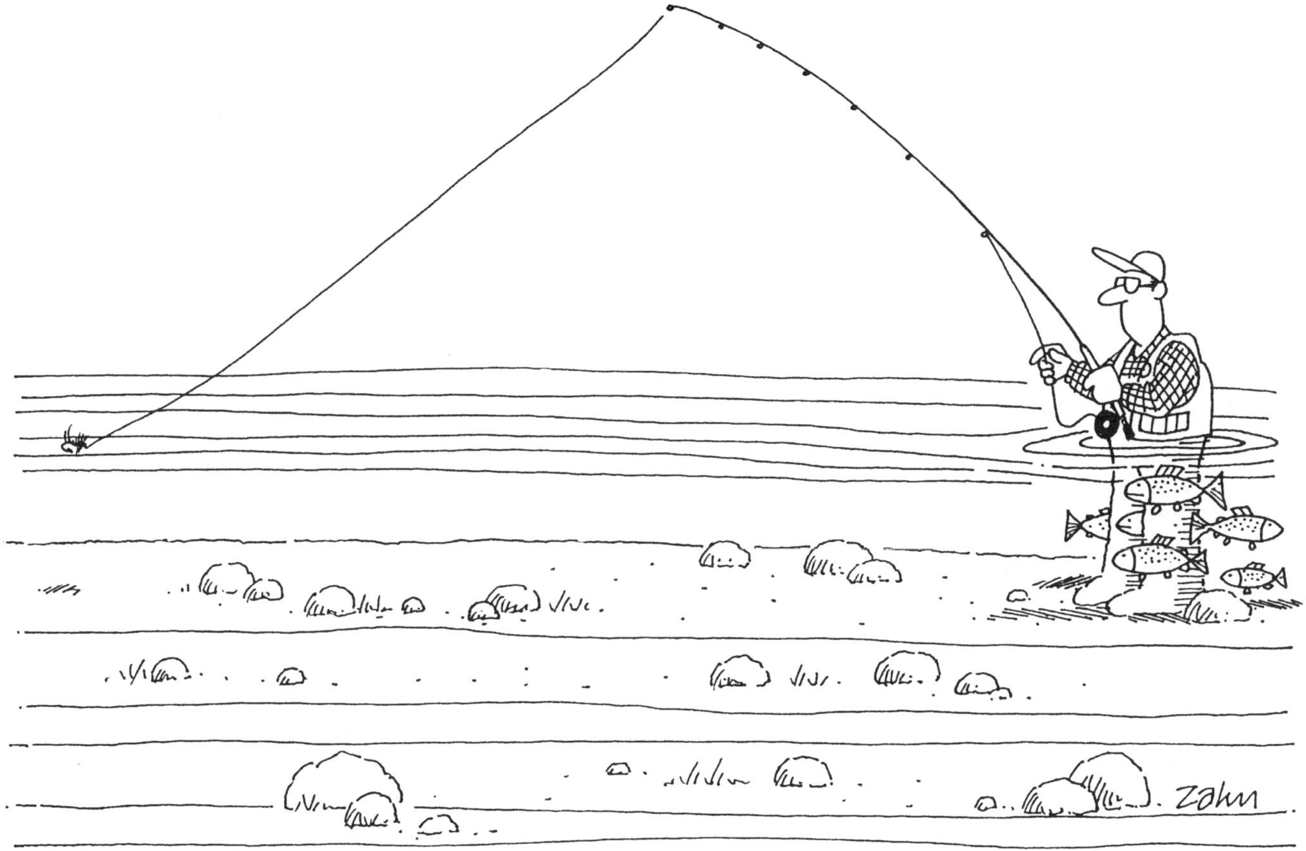
Zahn

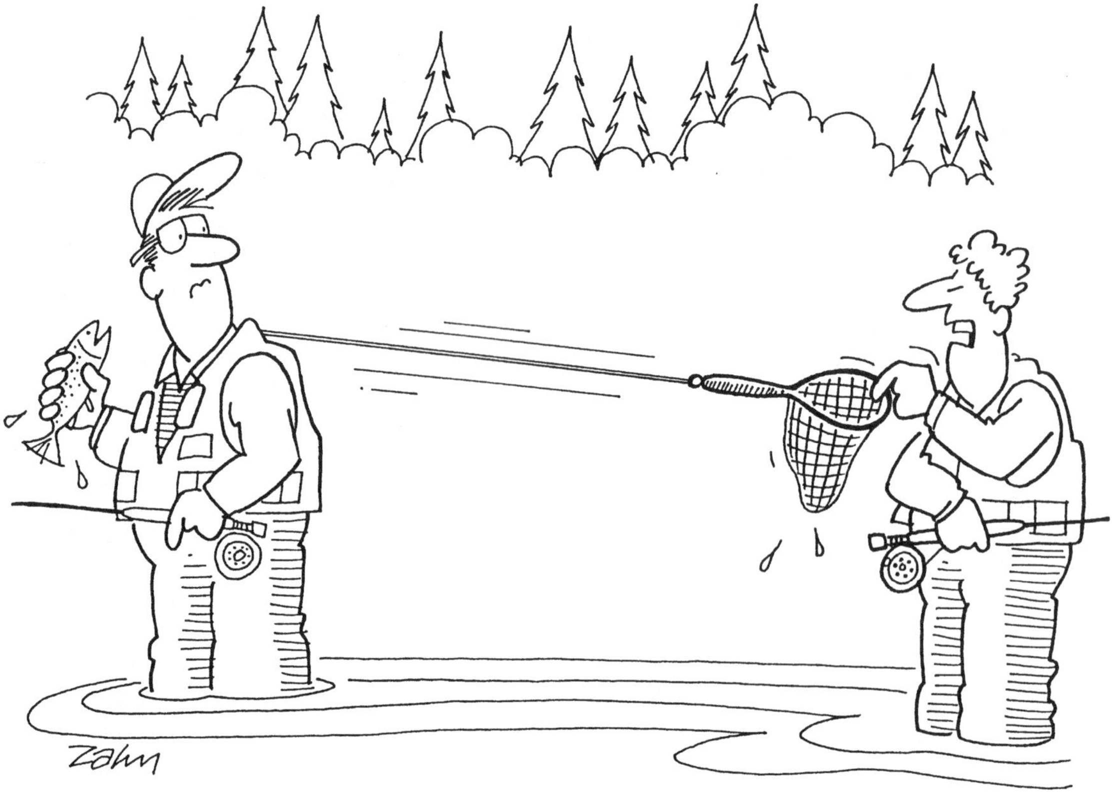
Zahn

" YOU HEARD ME...RELEASE HIM! "

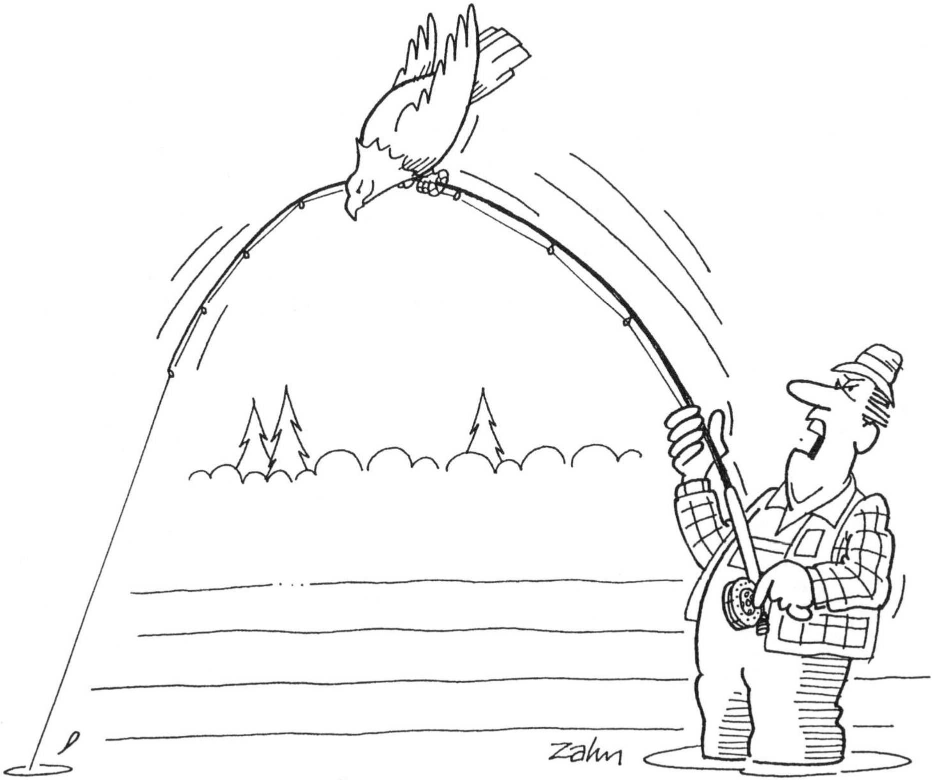
Zahn

"DON'T EVEN THINK ABOUT IT!"

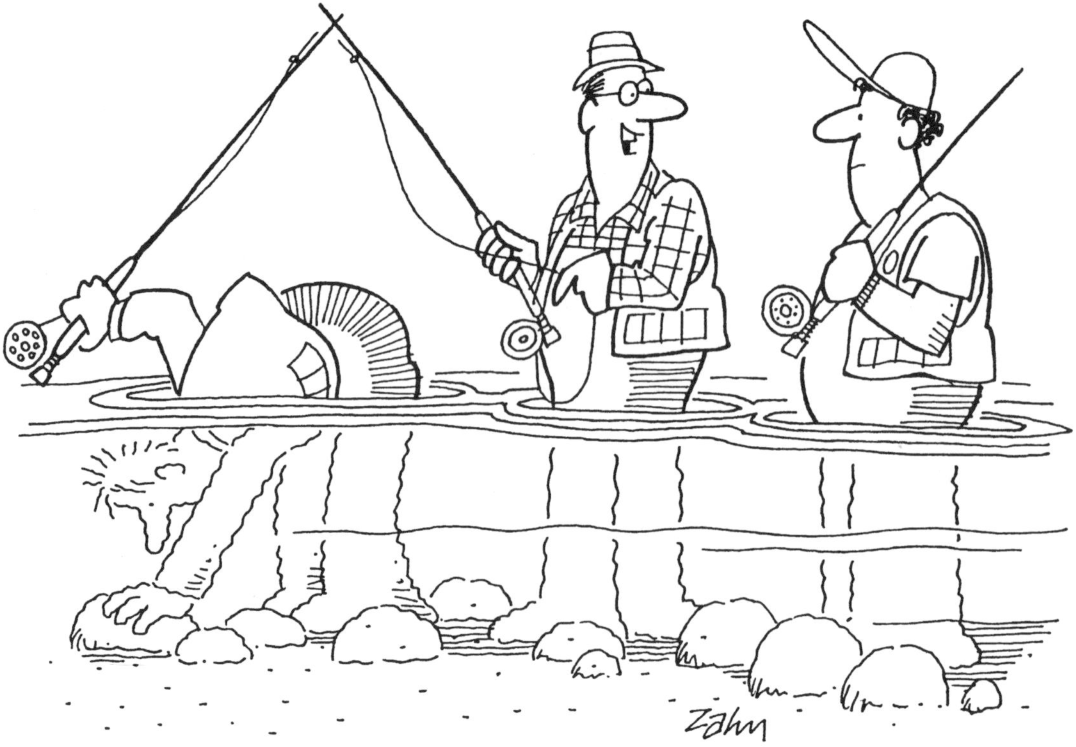
Zahn

"HE'S CHECKING THE LARVAE."

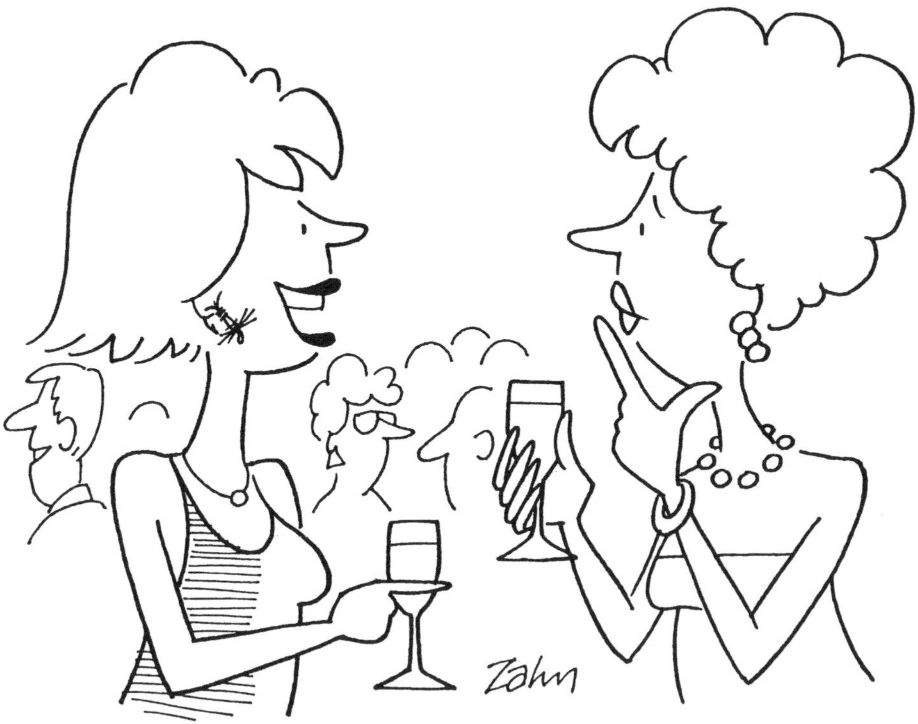
Zahn

"I COULDN'T FIND MY EARRINGS SO I USED A COUPLE OF MY HUSBAND'S TROUT FLIES!"

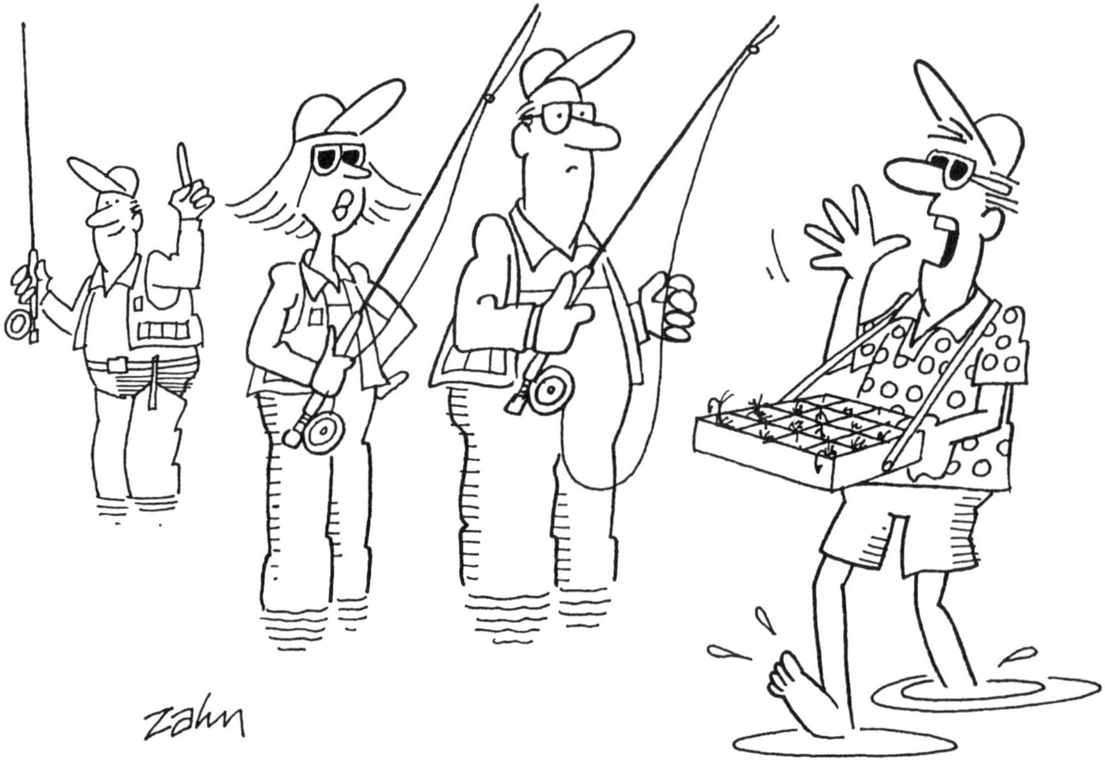
Zahn

"TROUT FLIES! GET YOUR TROUT FLIES HERE! TROUT FLIES!"

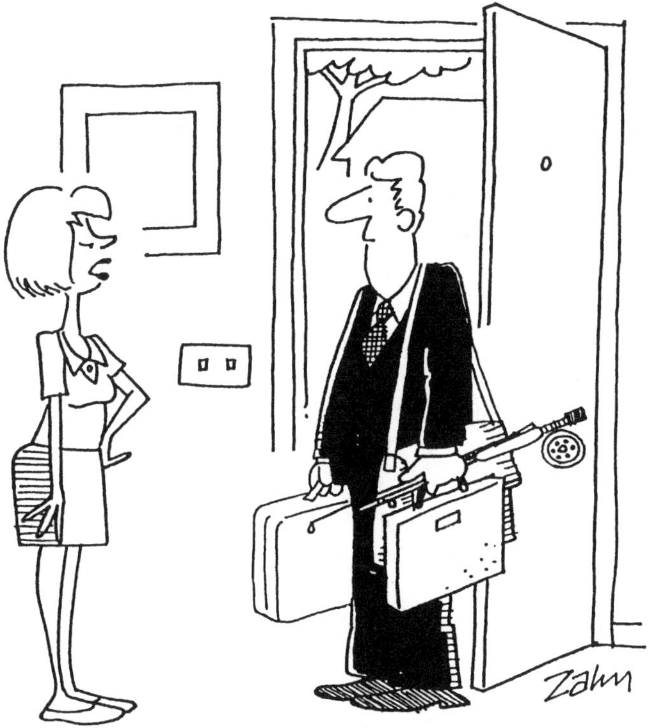
Zahm

"...BUT IF IT'S A BUSINESS TRIP WHY ARE YOU TAKING YOUR FLY POLE?"

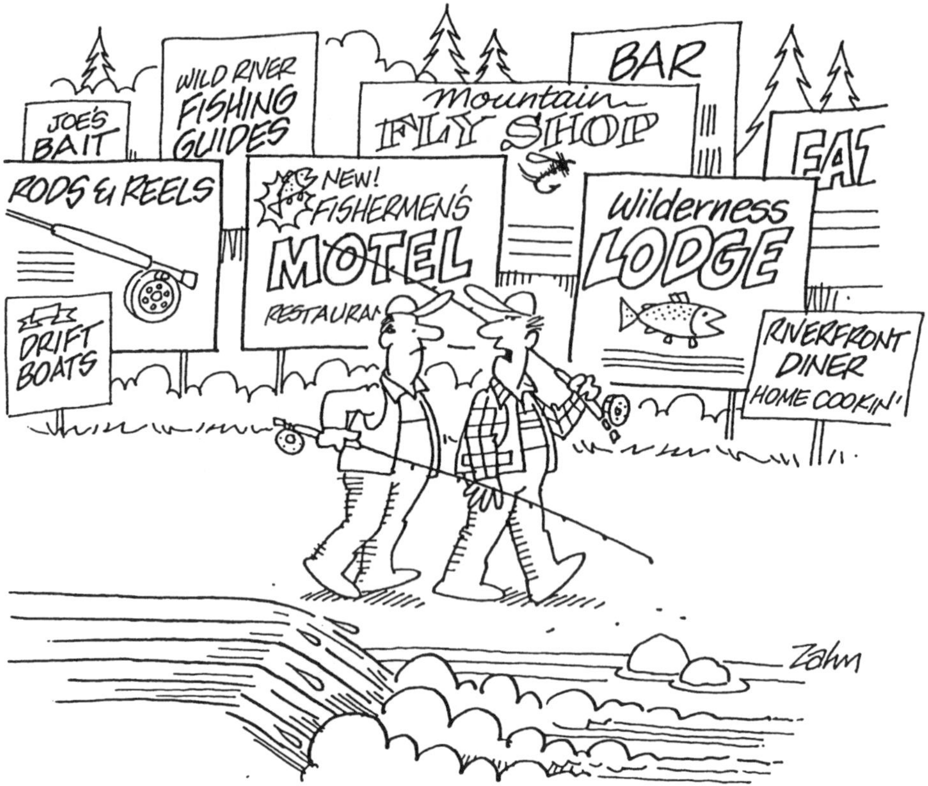
JOE'S BAIT
WILD RIVER FISHING GUIDES
BAR
Mountain FLY SHOP
RODS & REELS
NEW! FISHERMEN'S MOTEL
Wilderness LODGE
DRIFT BOATS
RIVERFRONT DINER HOME COOKIN'
Zahn

" WHO TOLD YOU THIS IS A 'VIRGIN' STREAM ? "

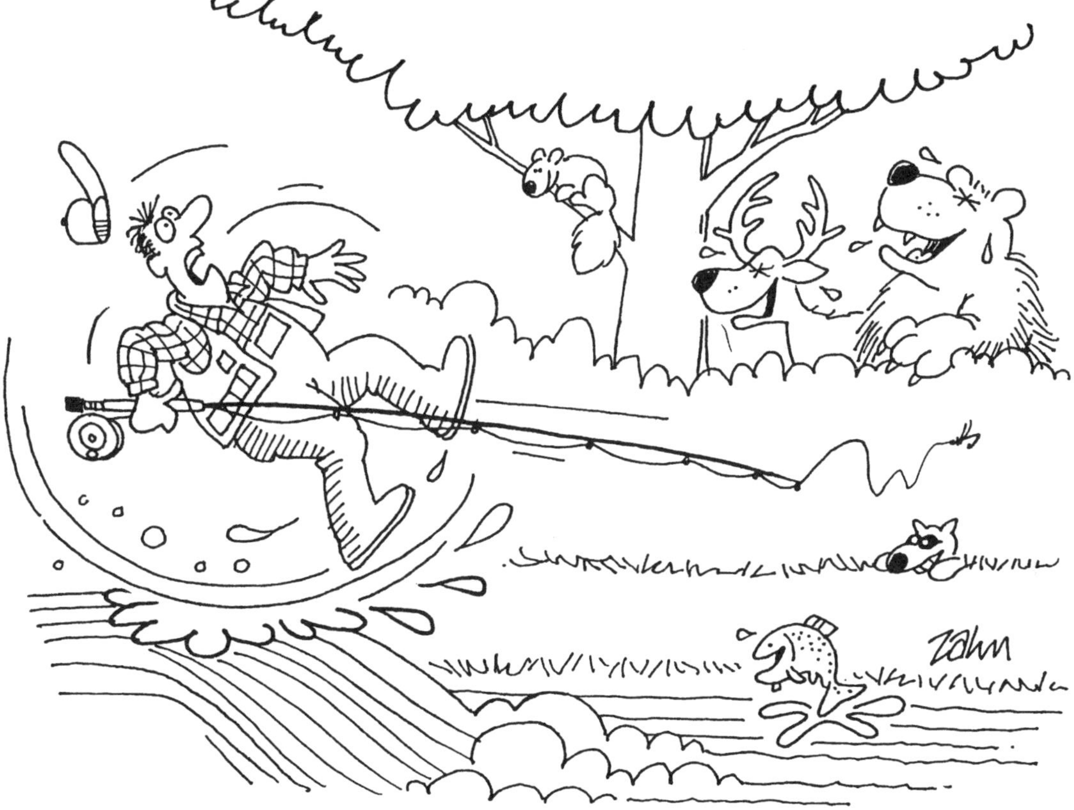
Zahn

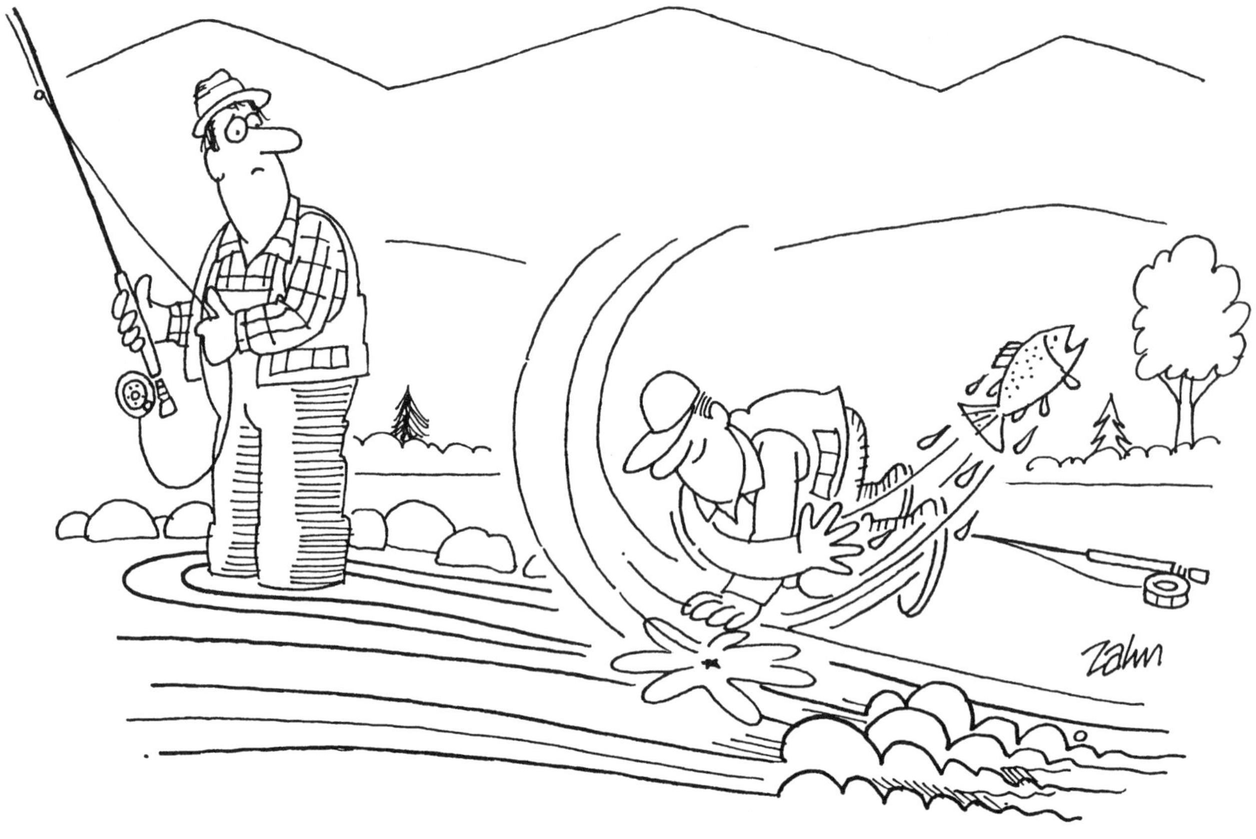
Zahn

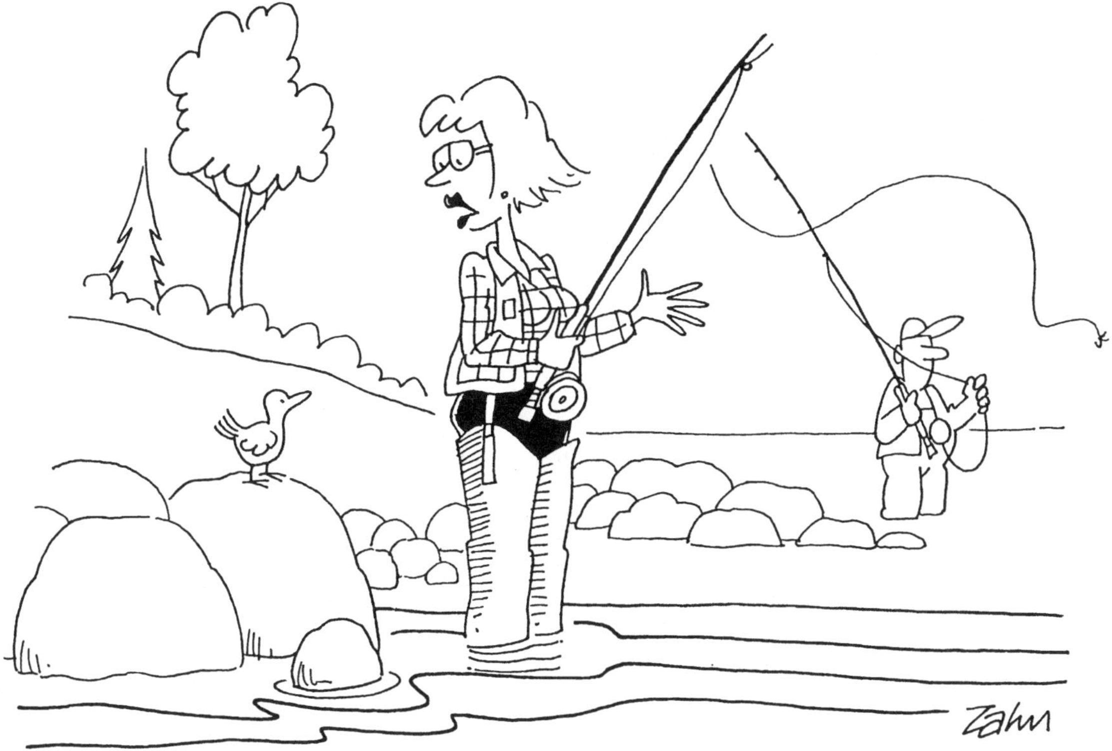
Zahn

"SORRY, I DON'T HAVE ANY WORMS."

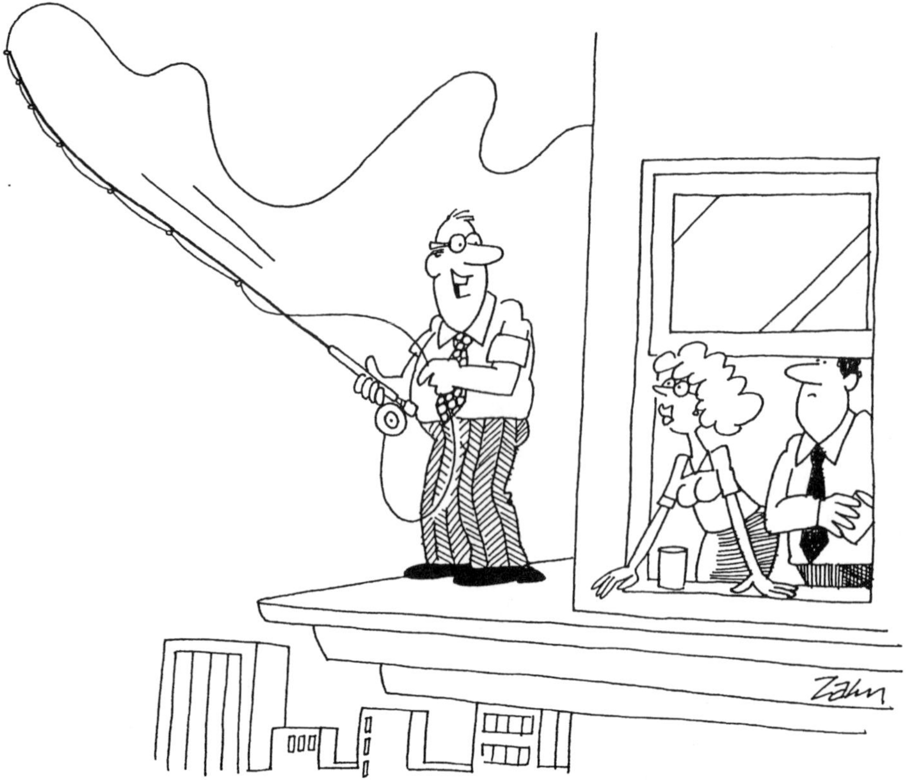
Zahn

"YOU DO WHAT YOU LIKE ON YOUR BREAK,
AND I'LL DO WHAT I LIKE ON MINE!"

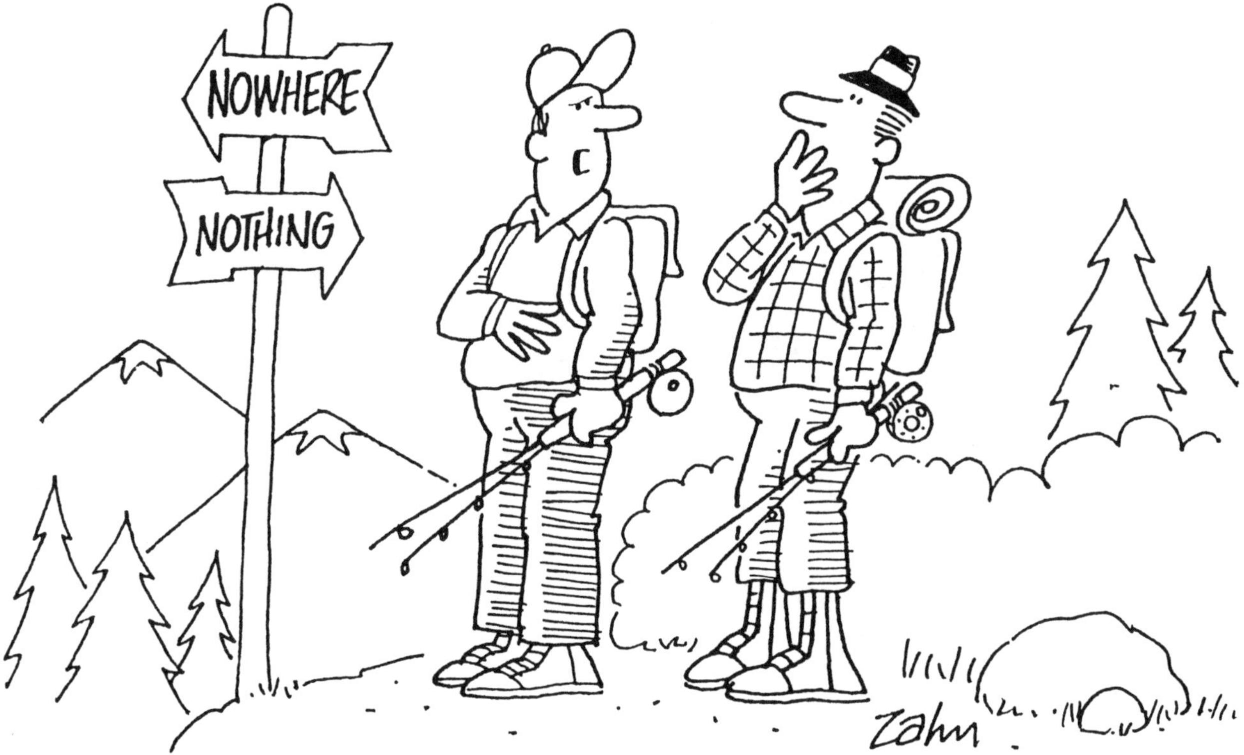
NOWHERE
NOTHING
Zahn

"ADMIT IT... YOU'RE LOST!"

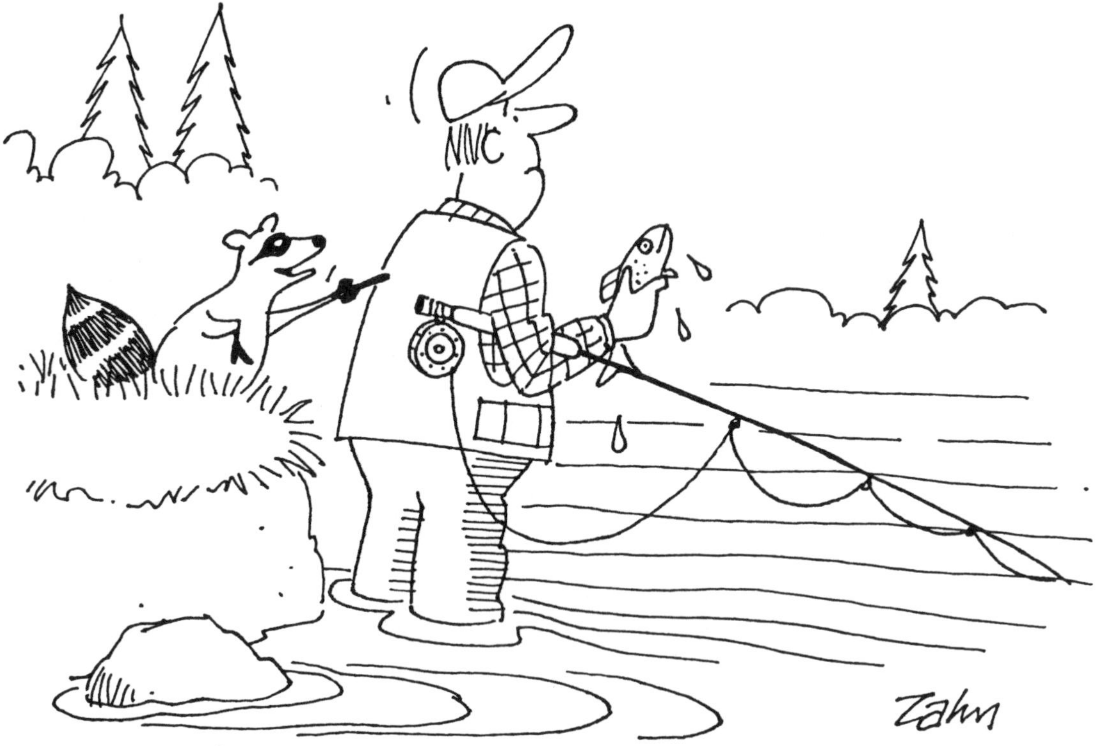
Zahn

"THIS IS A STICKUP! DON'T TURN AROUND; JUST HAND OVER THAT FISH!"

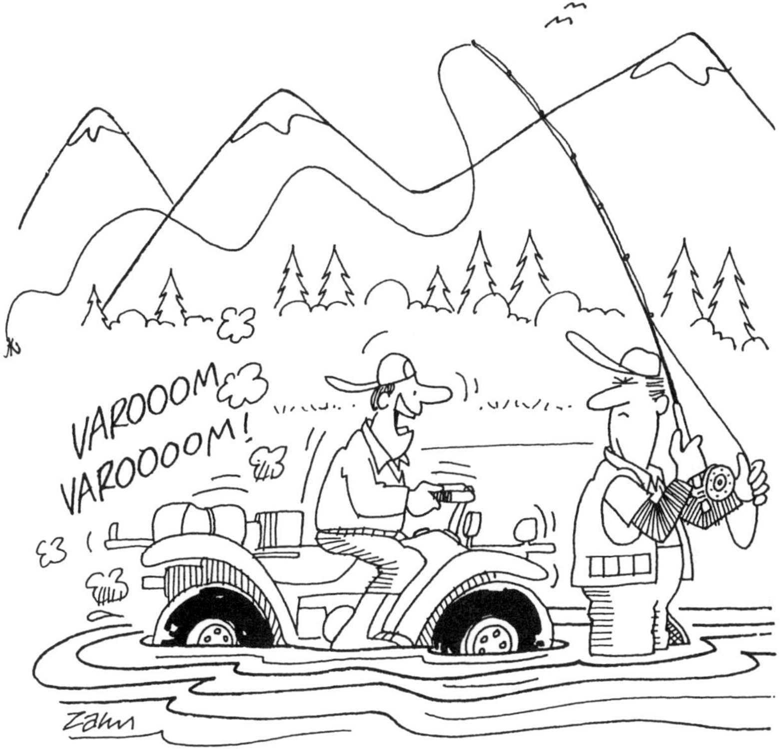
VAROOOM
VAROOOOM!
Zahn

"MAN! THIS IS REALLY ISOLATED COUNTRY, ISN'T IT?"

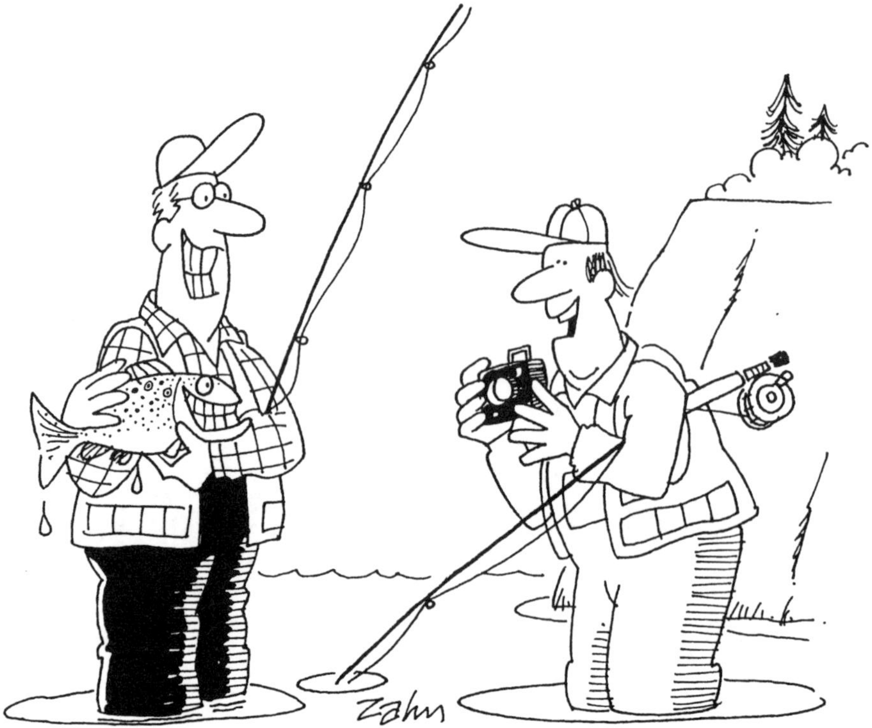
Zahn

"OKAY, NOW... GIVE US A BIG SMILE AND THEN WE'LL RELEASE YOU!"

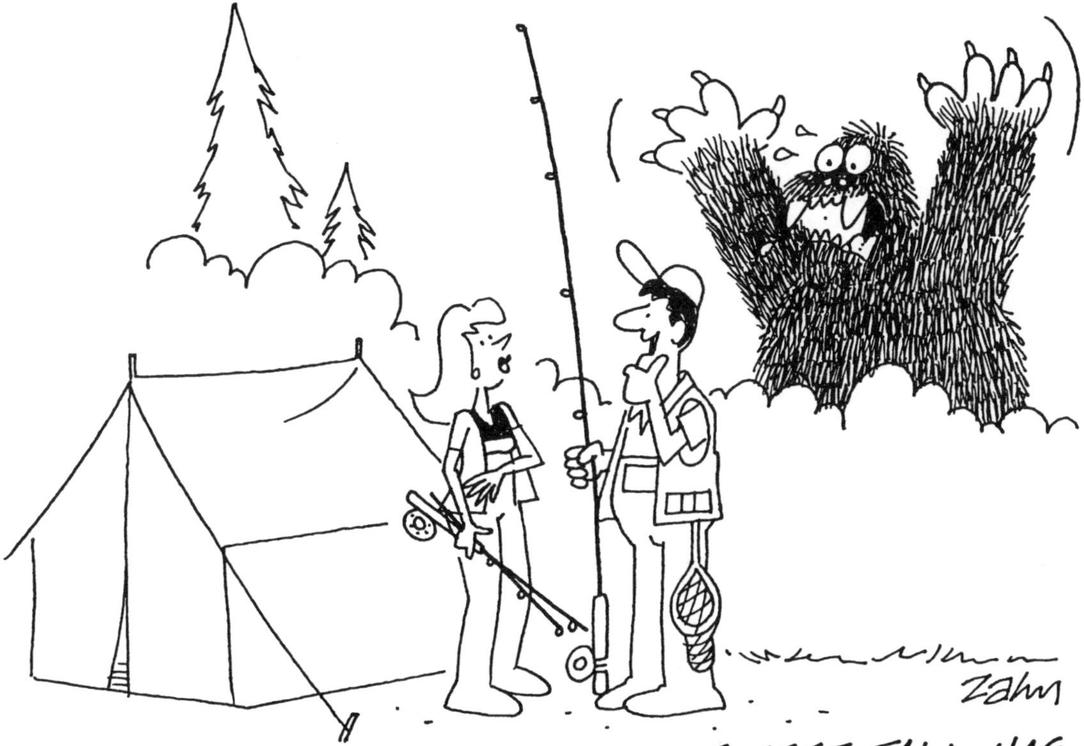
Zahn

"I GIVE UP... WHAT IS NINE FEET TALL, HAS TWO HUGE FANGS AND HAIR ALL OVER ITS BODY?"

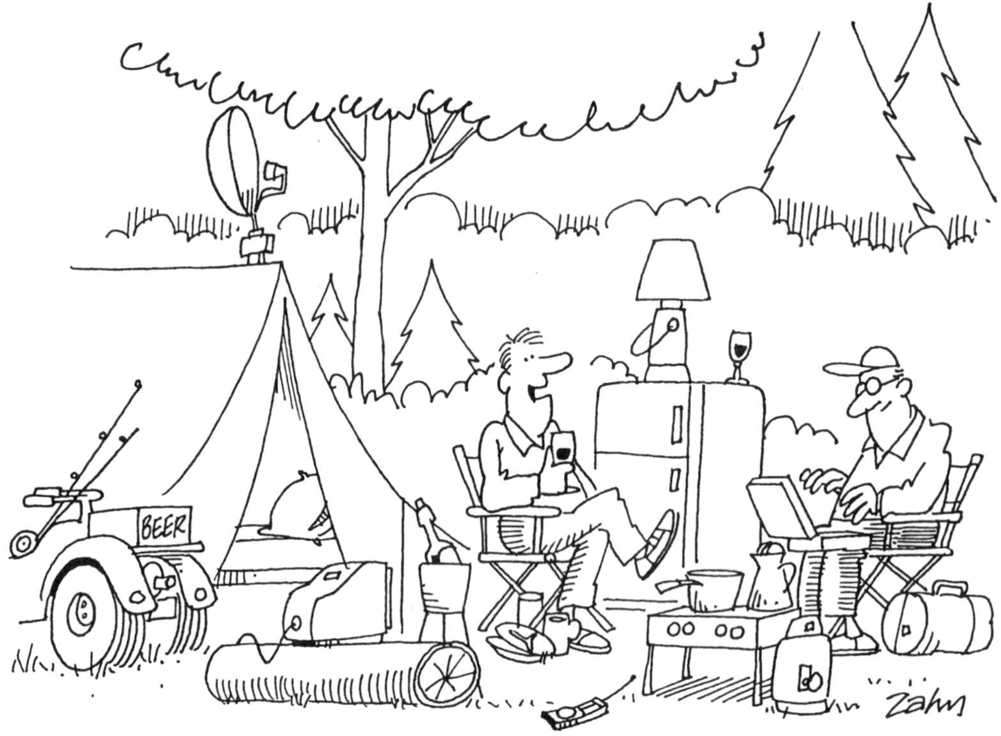

BEER
ZAHN

"I LOVE TO GET BACK TO NATURE AND ROUGH IT!"

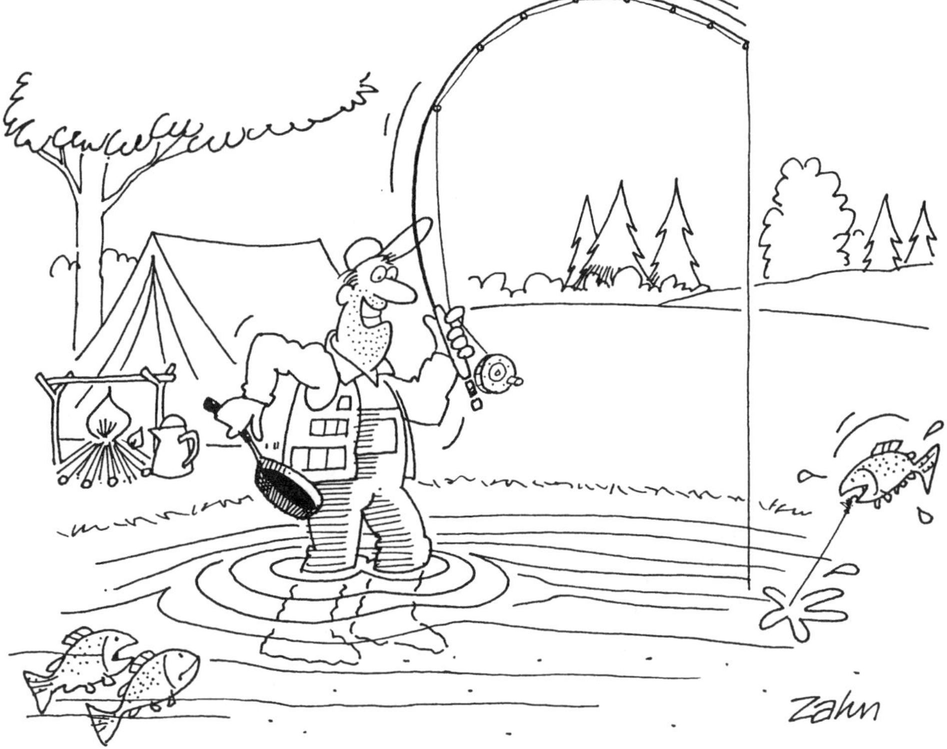
Zahn

"THIS GUY DEFINITELY DOESN'T PRACTICE CATCH AND RELEASE!"

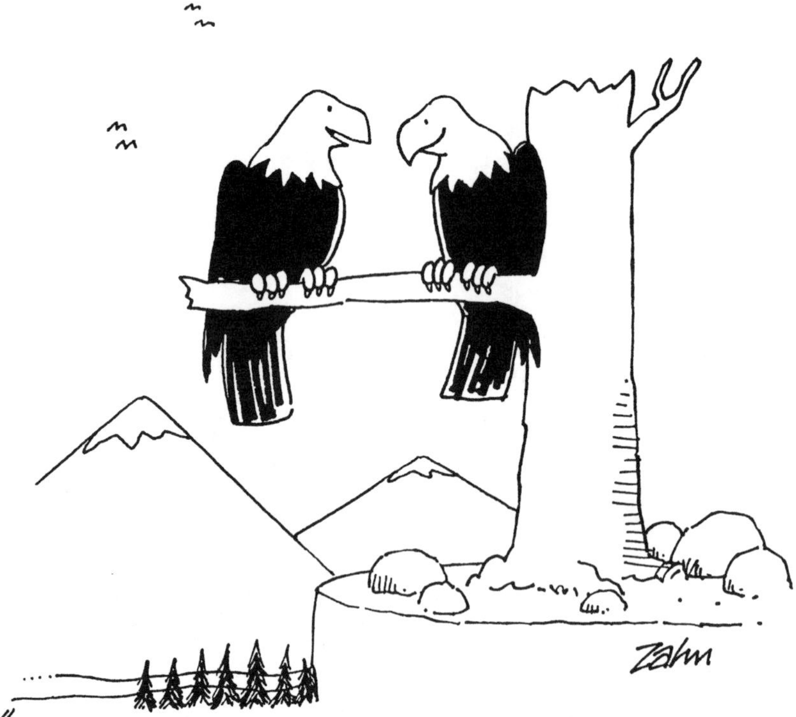
Zahm

"I SAW MY FIRST BROWN-VESTED FLY FISHERMAN OF THE YEAR THIS MORNING... THAT'S A SURE SIGN OF THE BEGINNING OF THE SALMON RUN."

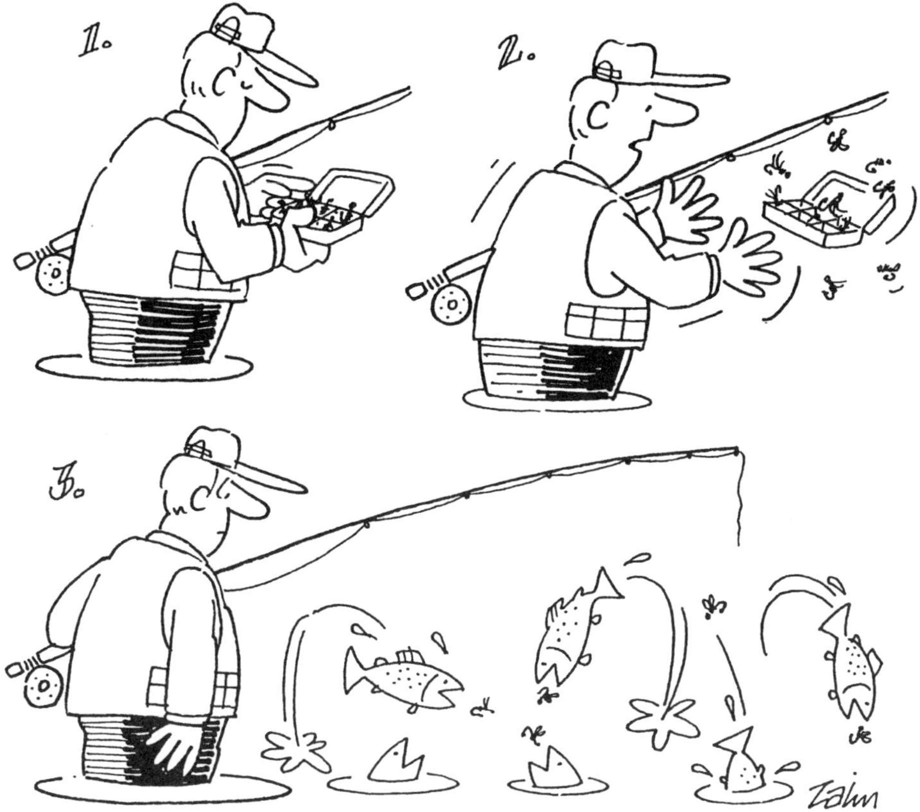
1.
2.
3.
Zahn

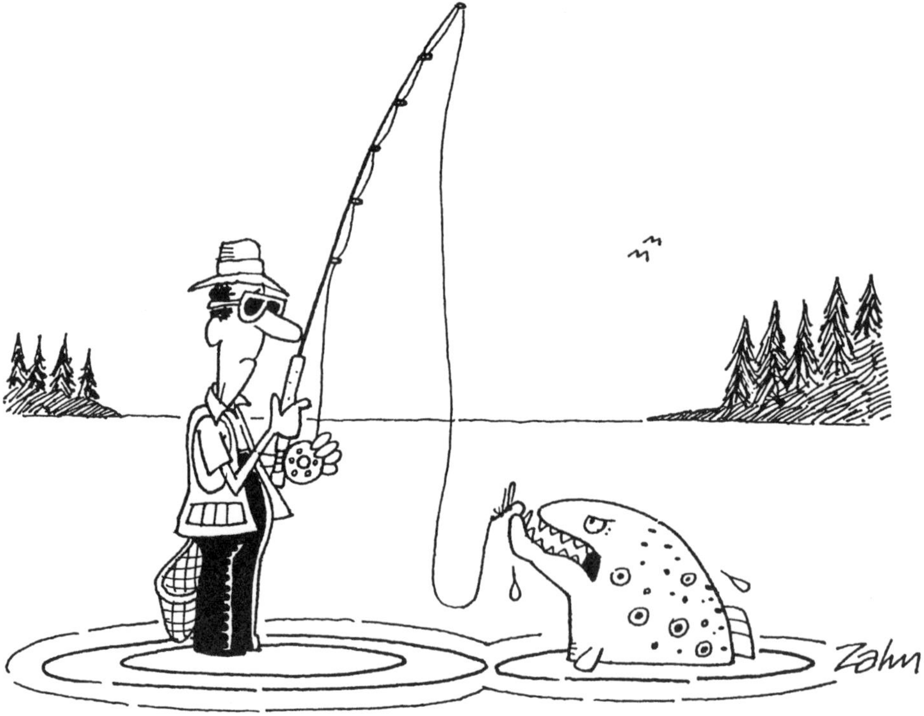
Zahn

" JUST REACH DOWN AND GENTLY REMOVE THE HOOK, AND I'LL LET YOU GO THIS TIME."

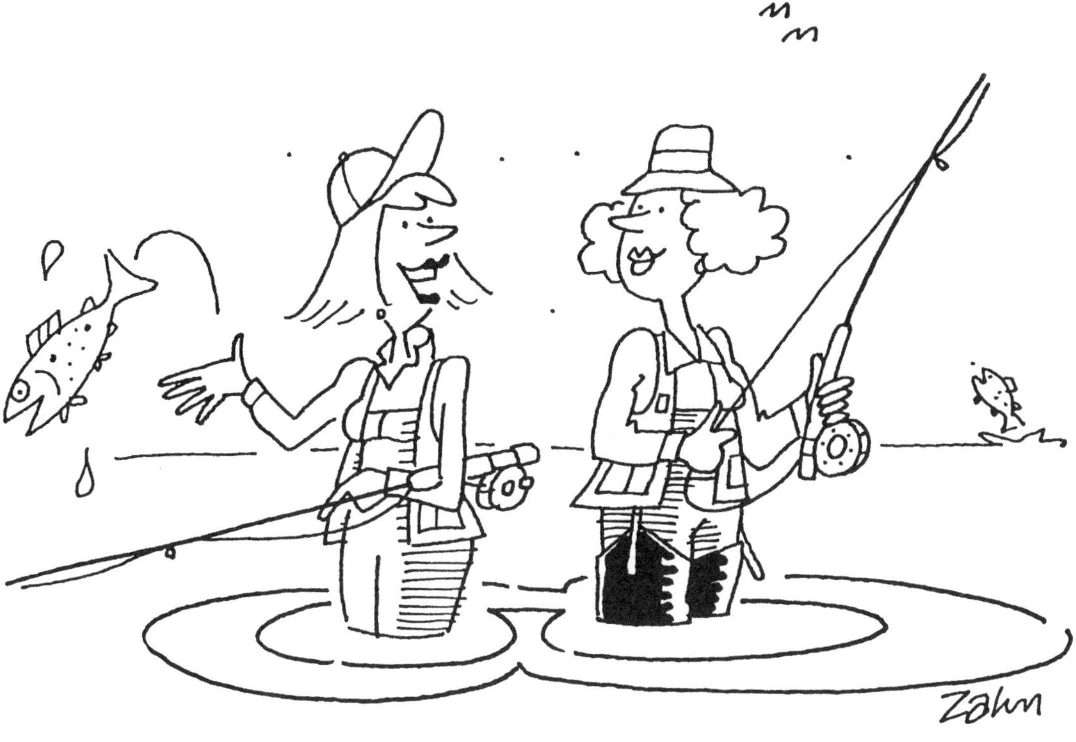
Zahn

"I PRACTICE CATCH AND RELEASE WITH FISH AND MEN."

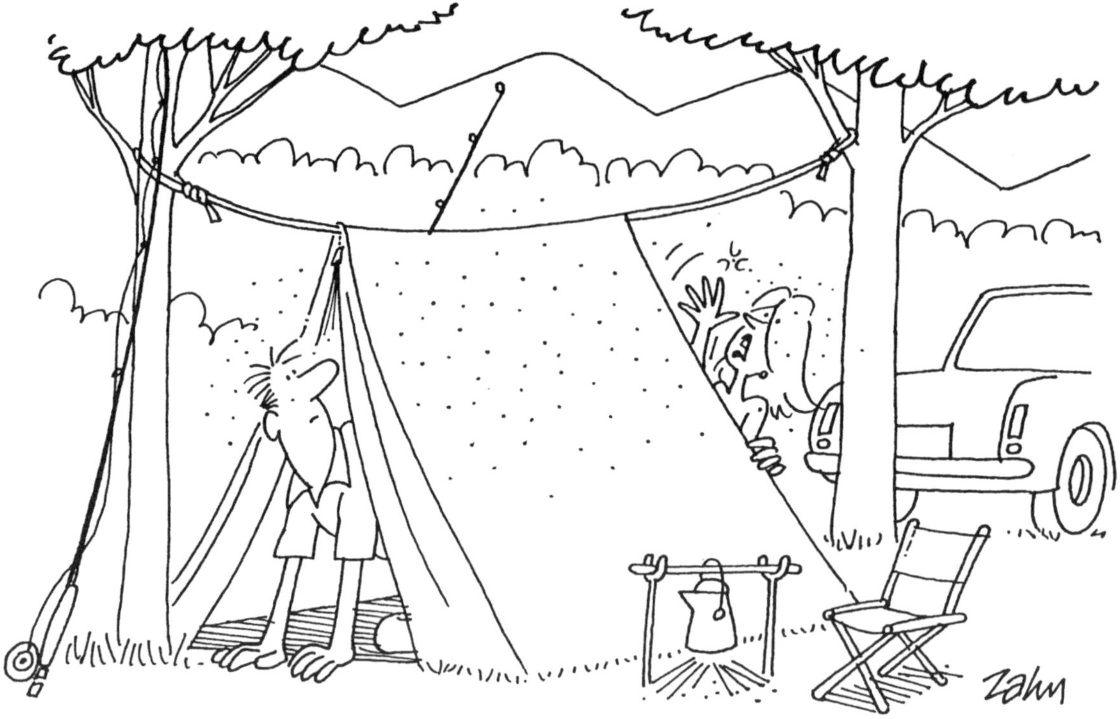
Zahn

"I THINK THE HATCH IS MOSTLY DEERFLIES, HORSEFLIES, BLACKFLIES, AND MOSQUITOES!"

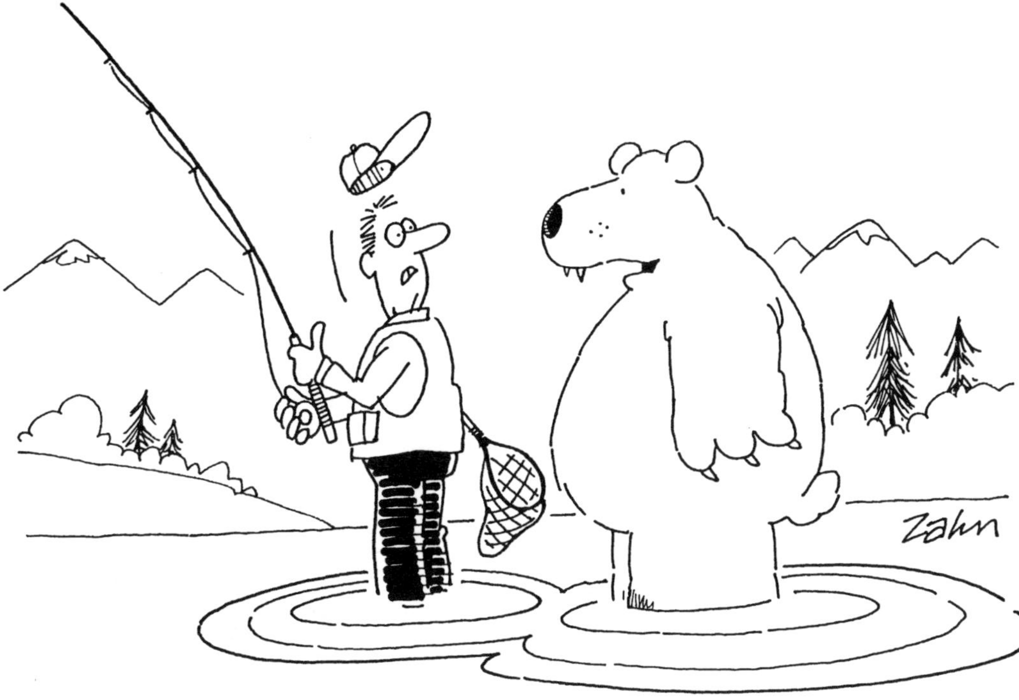
Zahn

"ANY LUCK ?"

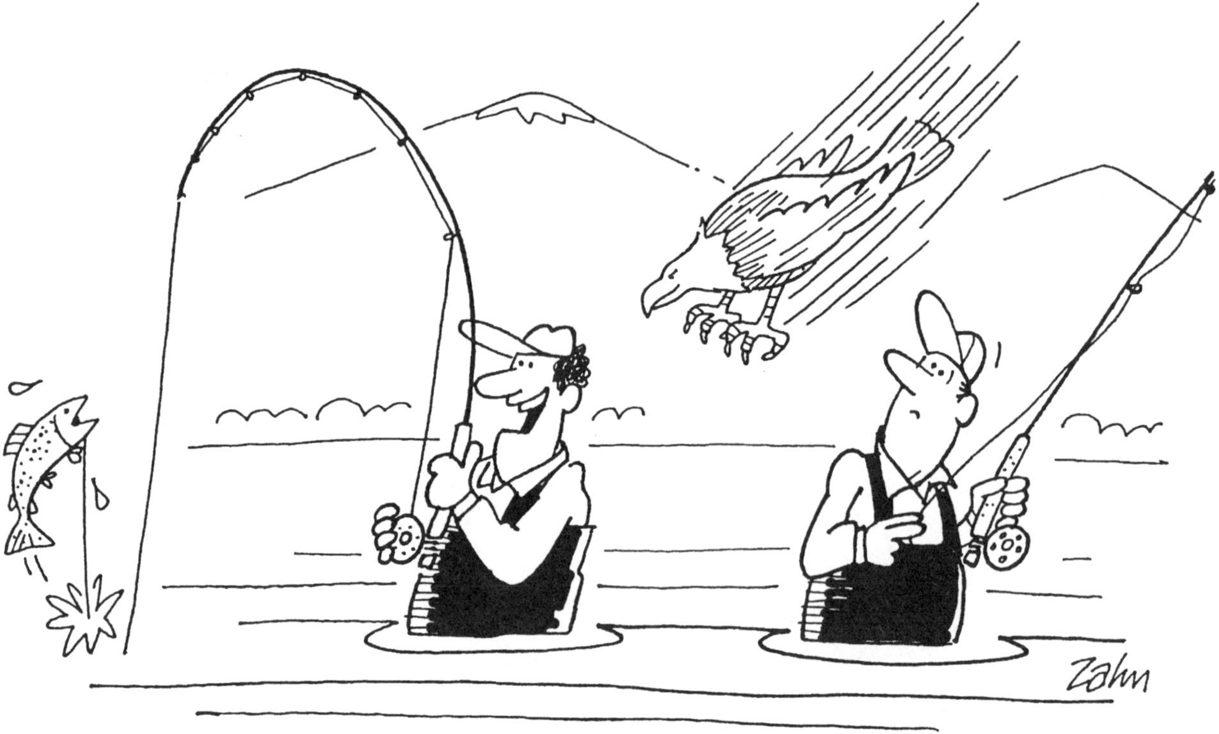
Zahn

"FINALLY! AFTER THREE DAYS OF FISHING, I'VE GOT A BEAUTY!"

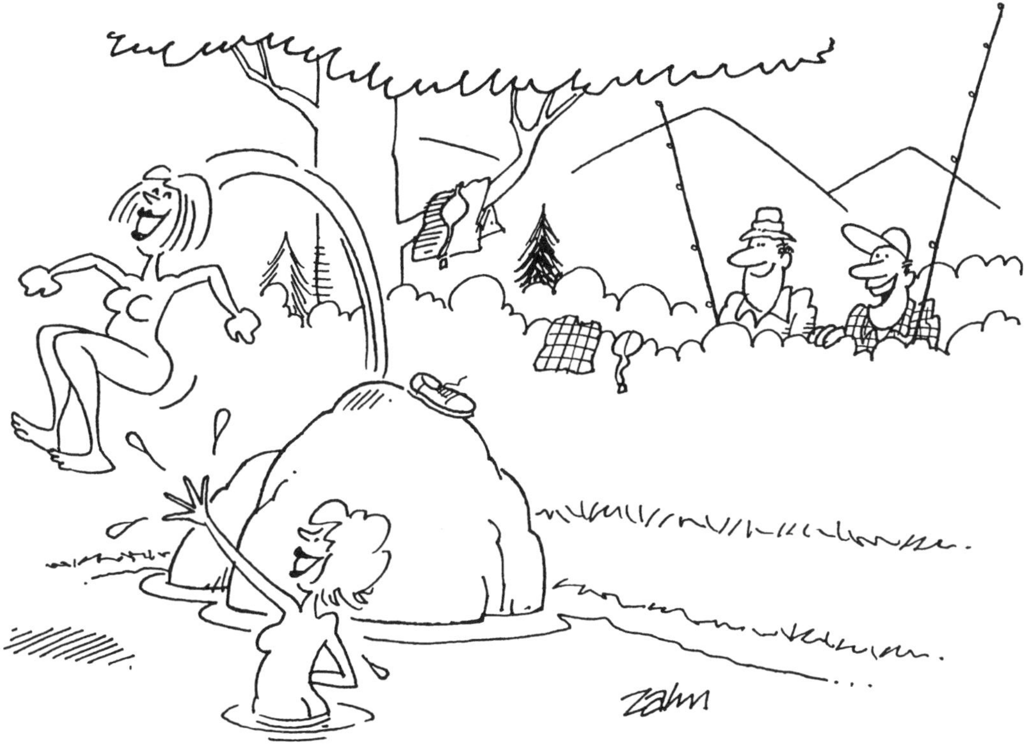
zahn

"GOD! I LOVE NATURE!"

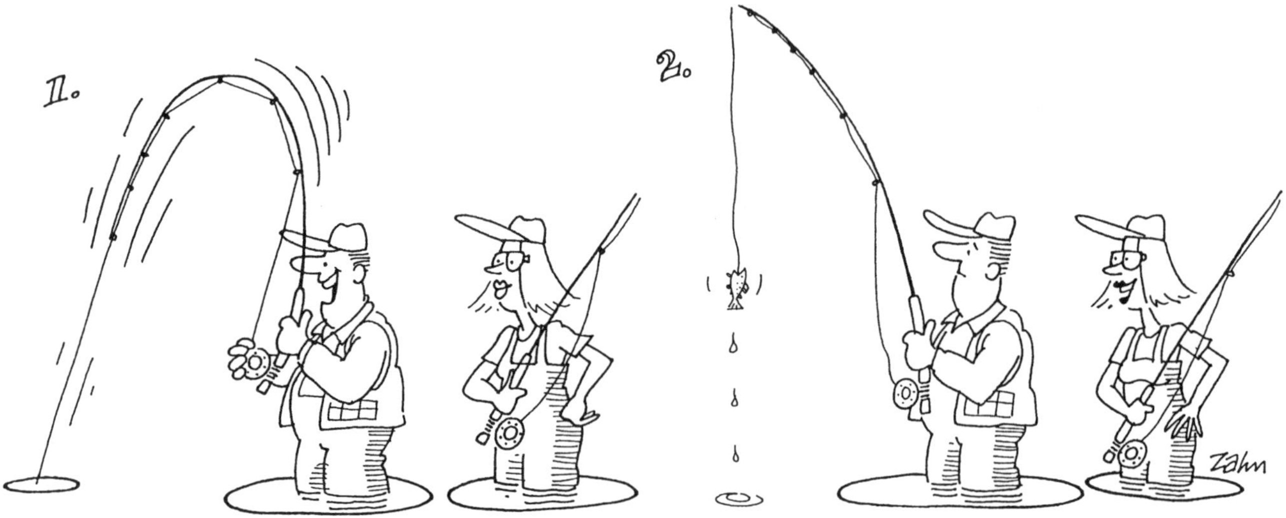
1.
2.
Zahn

"WOW! HE'S EITHER HUGE OR ONE HELL OF A FIGHTER!"

"ONE HELL OF A FIGHTER."

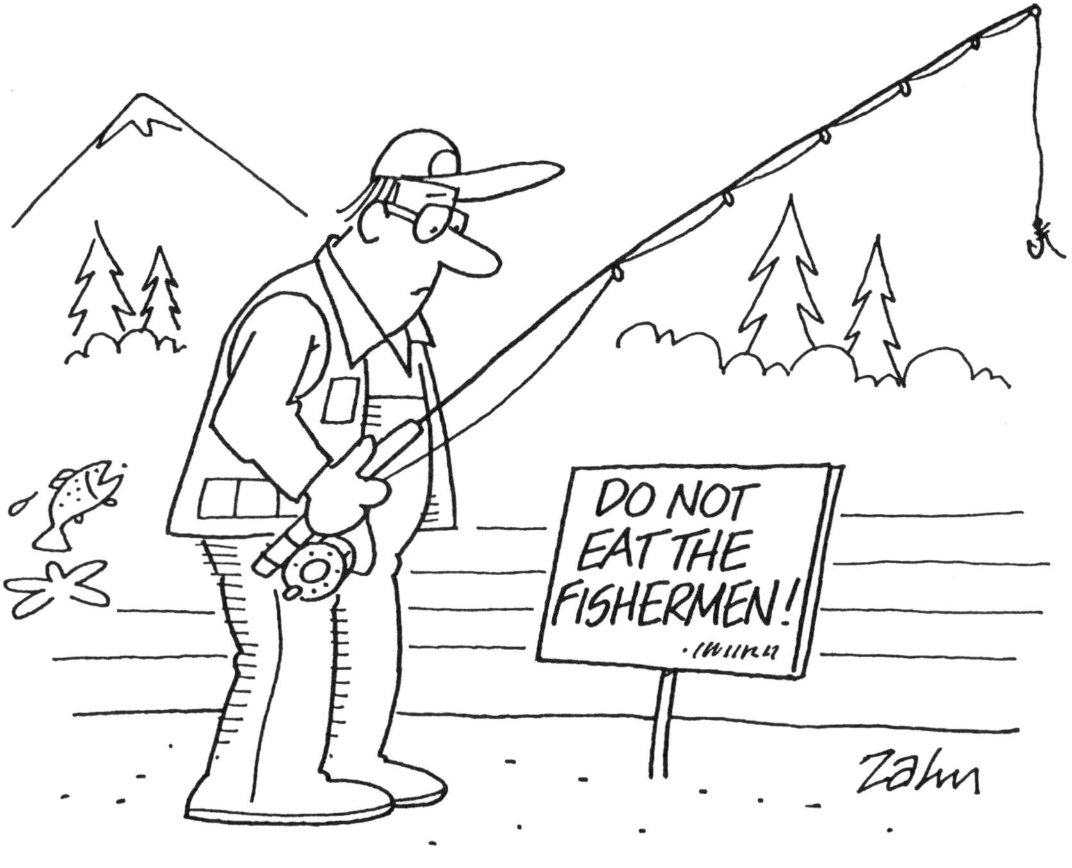
DO NOT
EAT THE
FISHERMEN!
Zahn

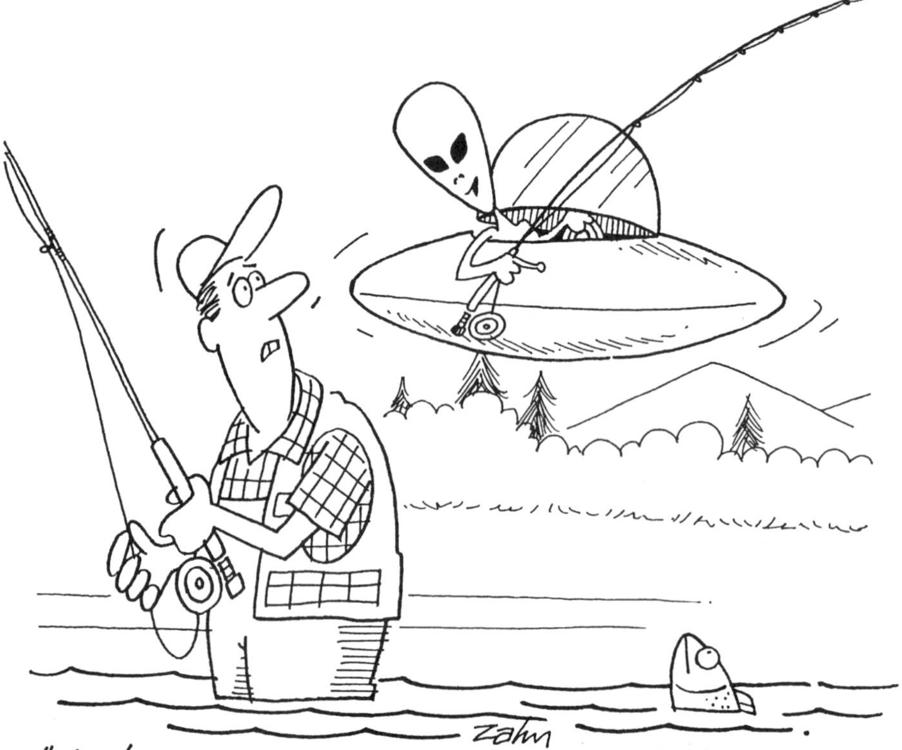
Zahn

"HOW'S THE FLY-FISHING HERE?"

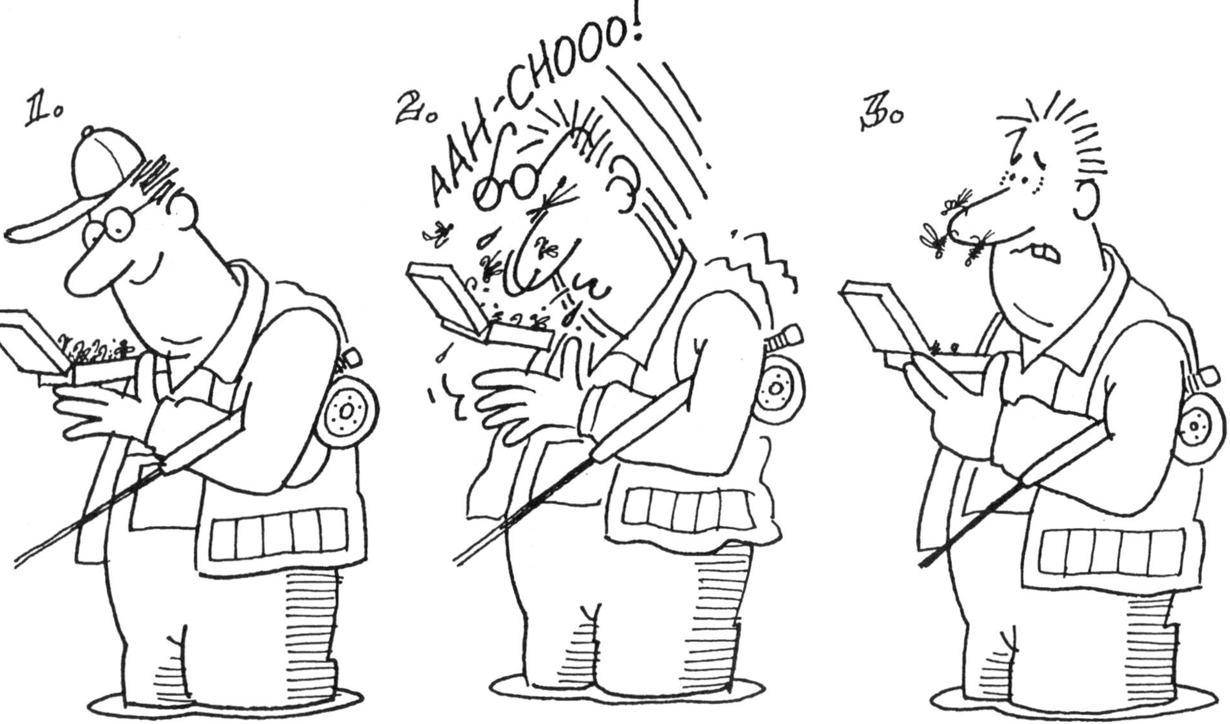
1.
2.
AAH-CHOOO!
3.

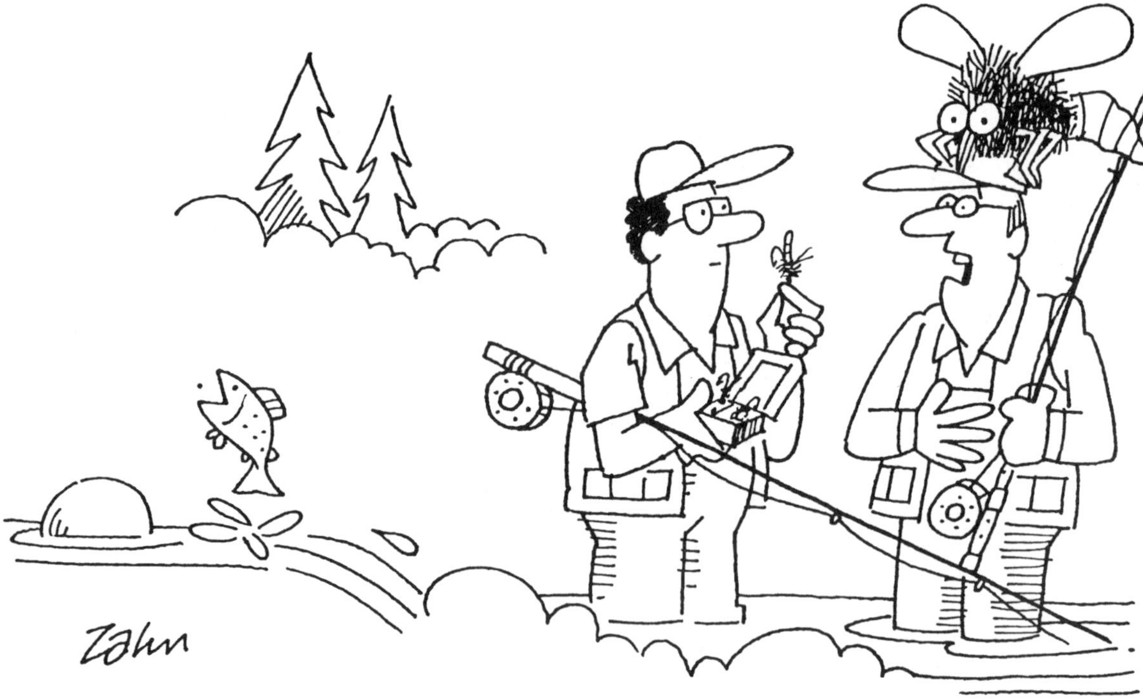
Zahn

"NEVER MIND TRYING TO MATCH THE HATCH...
LET'S GET THE HECK OUT OF HERE!"

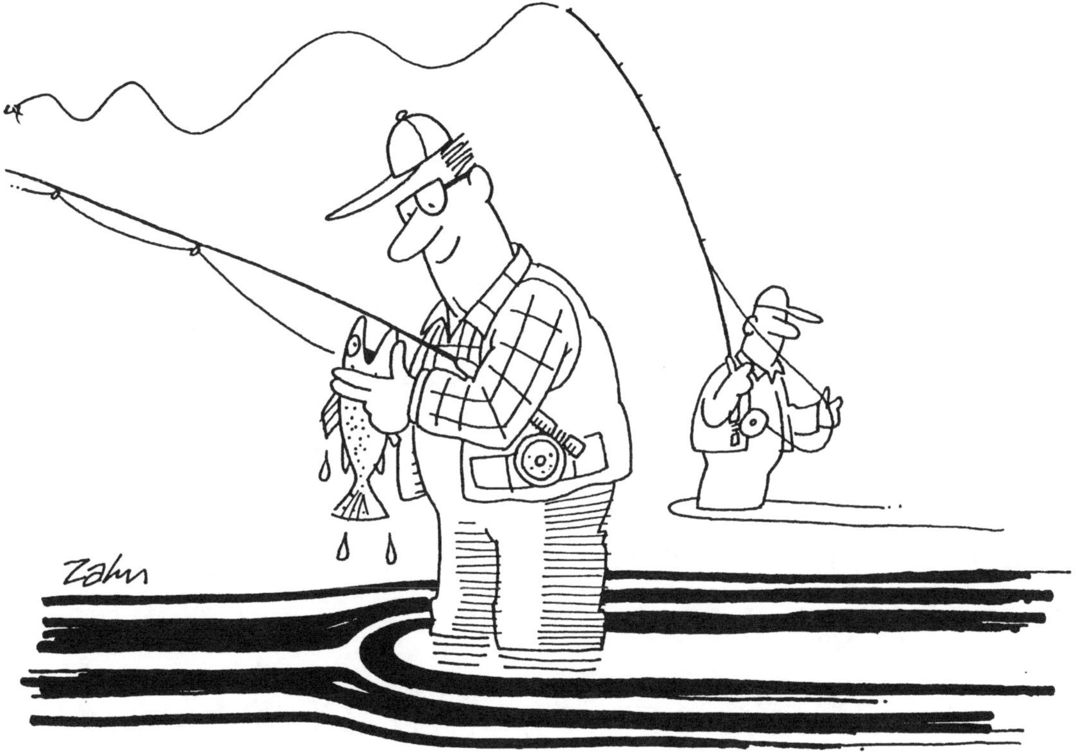
Zahn

"♪ PLEASE RELEASE MEEEE... LET ME GOOOO ♪"

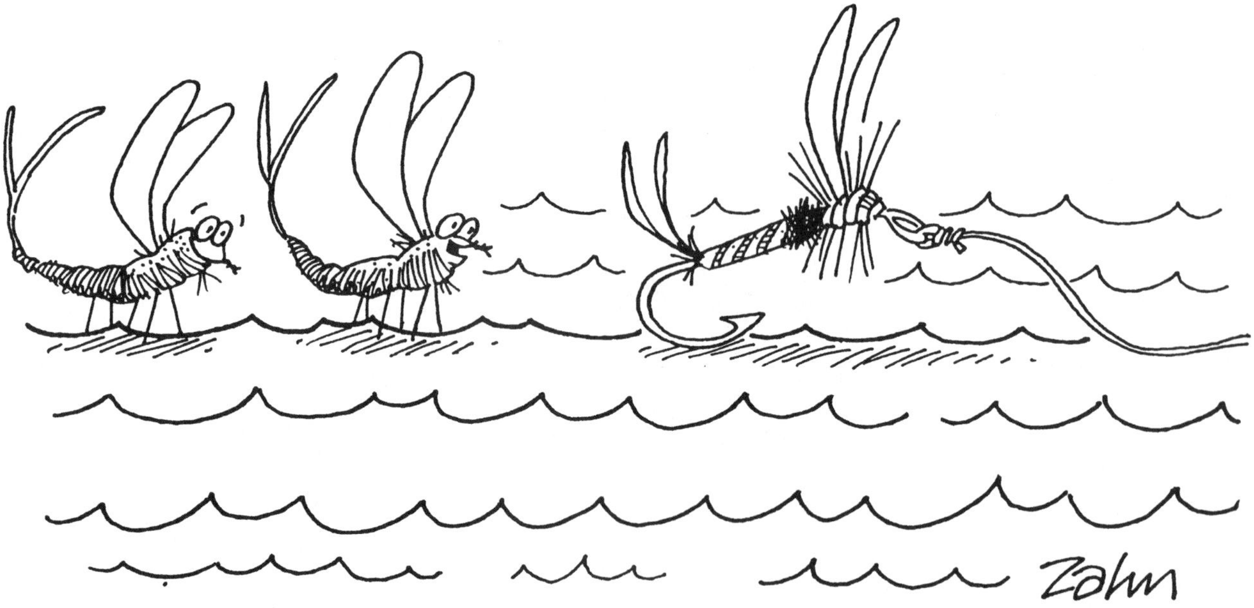
Zahn

"WOW! LOOK AT THE BUILD ON HIM!"

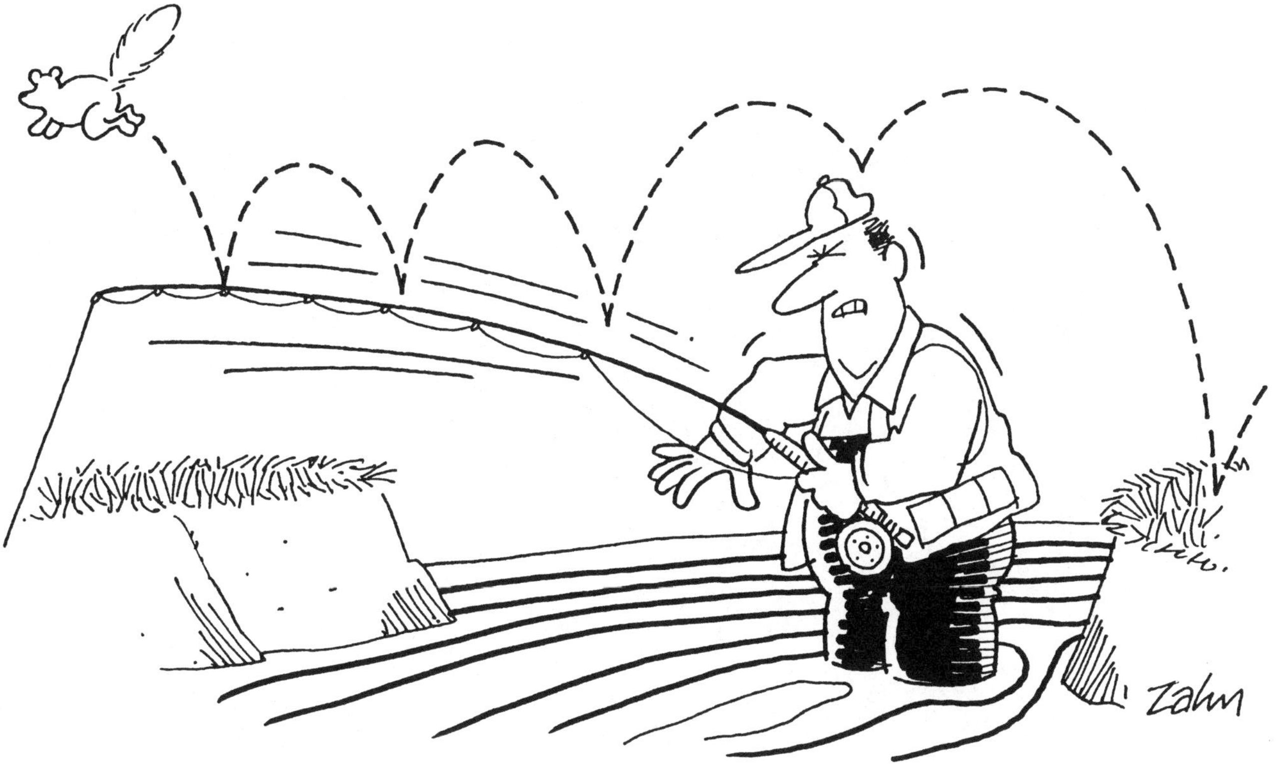
Zahn

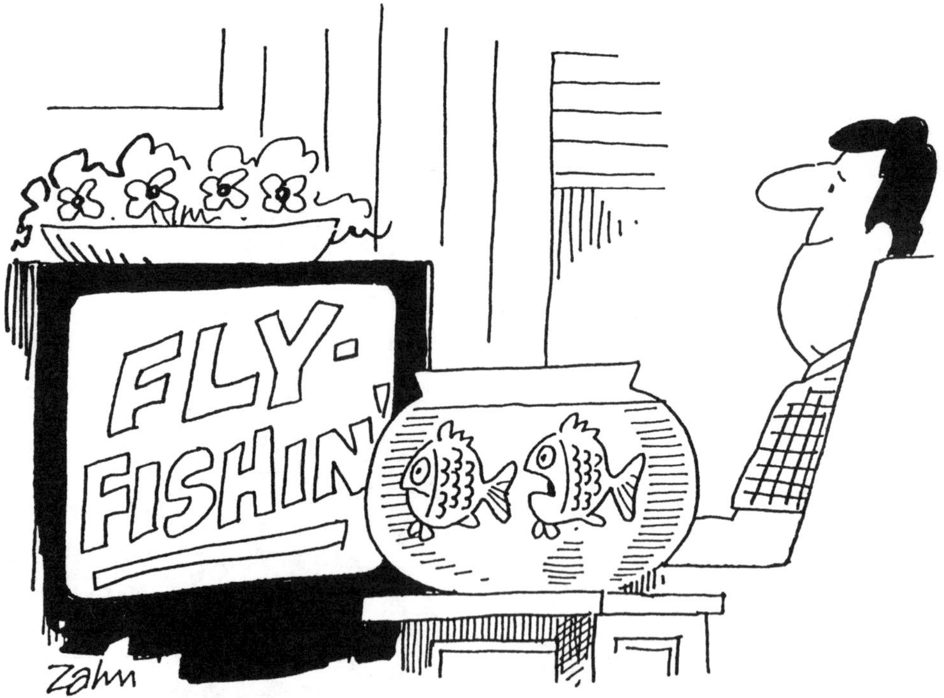
FLY-FISHIN'
Zahn

"OH, NO! ANOTHER HORROR MOVIE!"

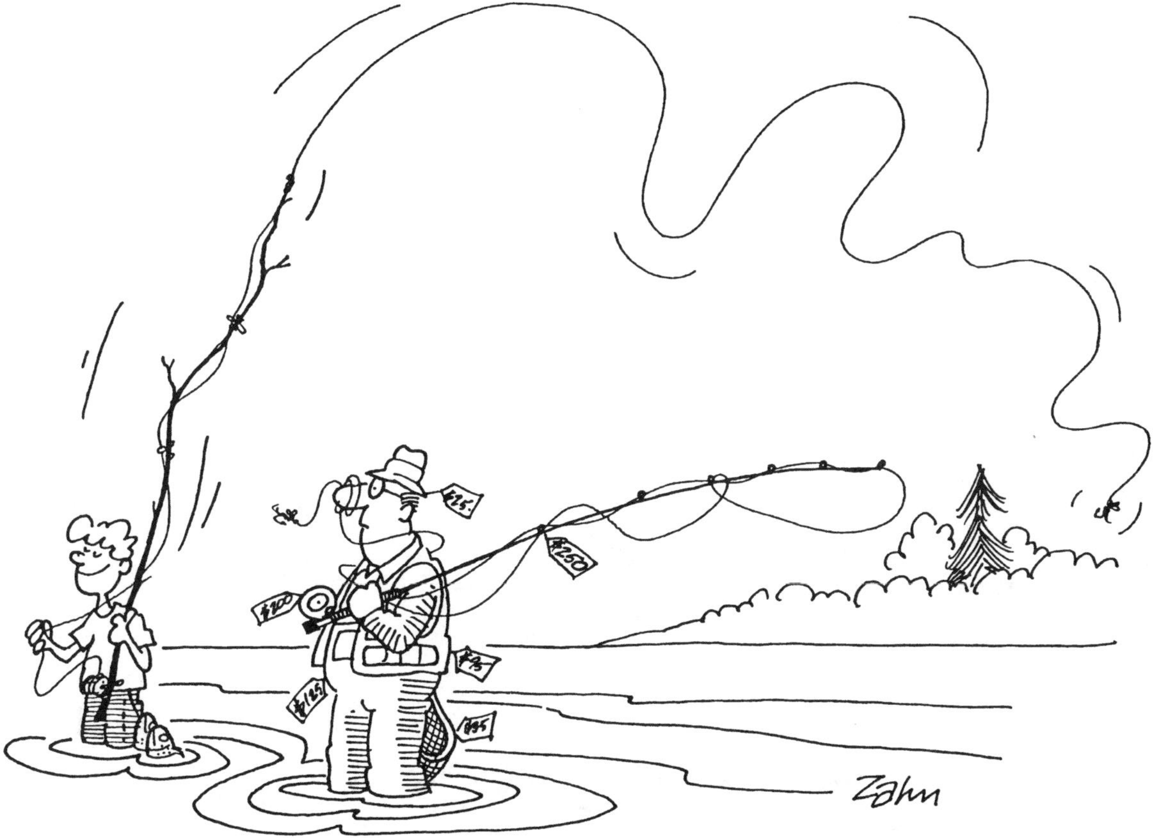
$25.
$250
$200
$75
$125
Zahn

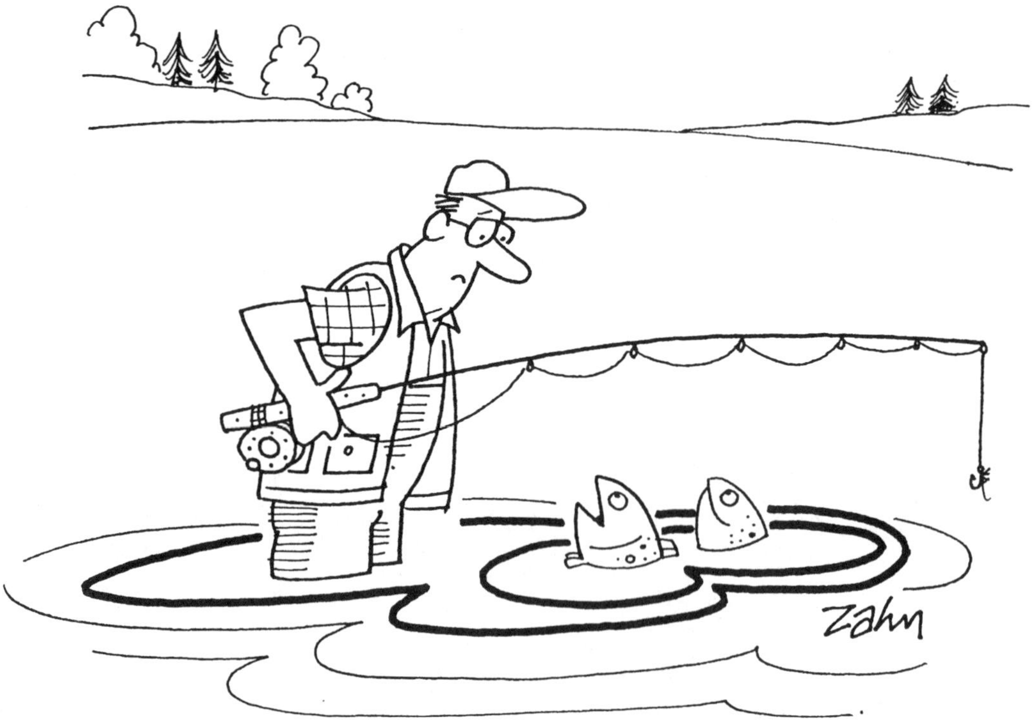
Zahn

"THANK YOU FOR YOUR SUBMISSION, BUT WE'RE SORRY TO SAY WE FIND IT UNACCEPTABLE."

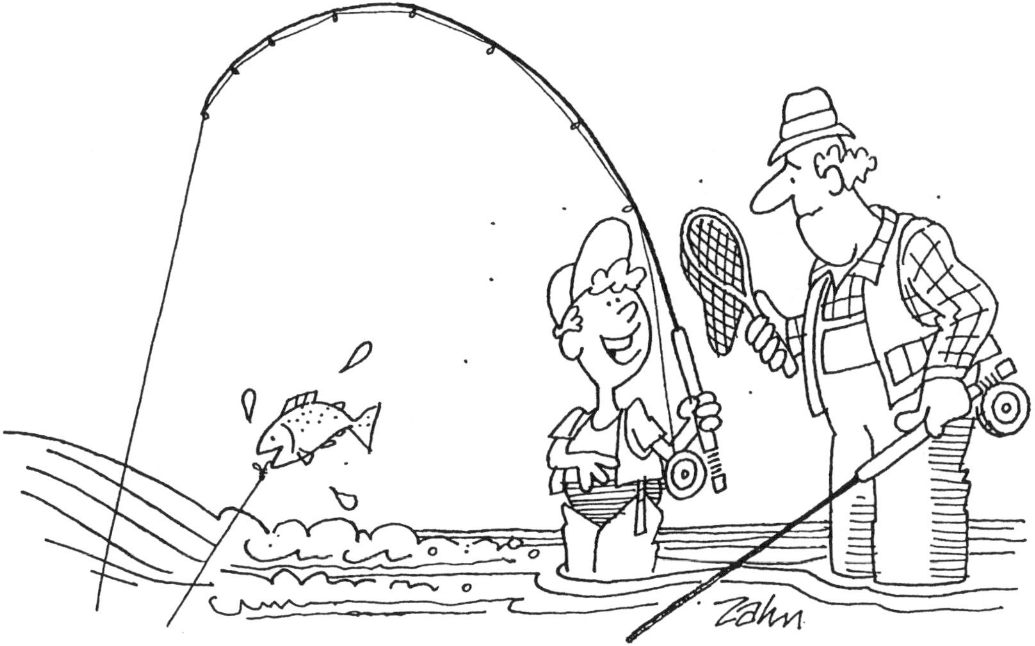
Zahn

"I'VE BEEN CATCHING THEM ALL DAY LONG, DAD, WOULD YOU LIKE TO LAND ONE ?"

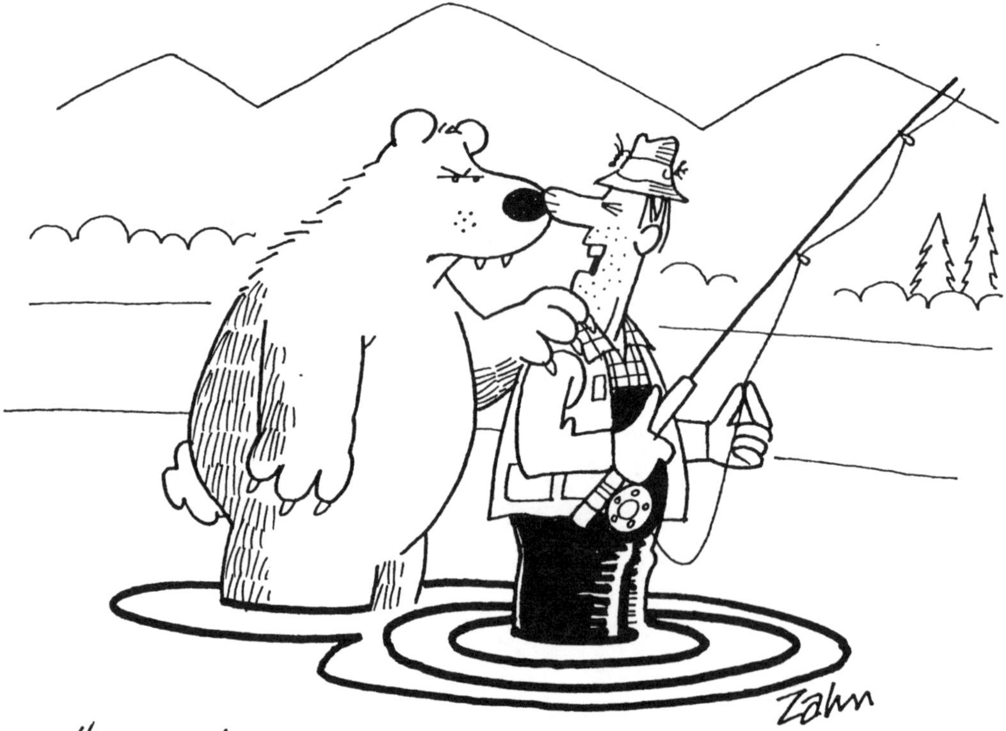
Zahn

"I CAN'T BELIEVE I LEFT MY GLASSES BACK AT CAMP THIS MORNING, ED."

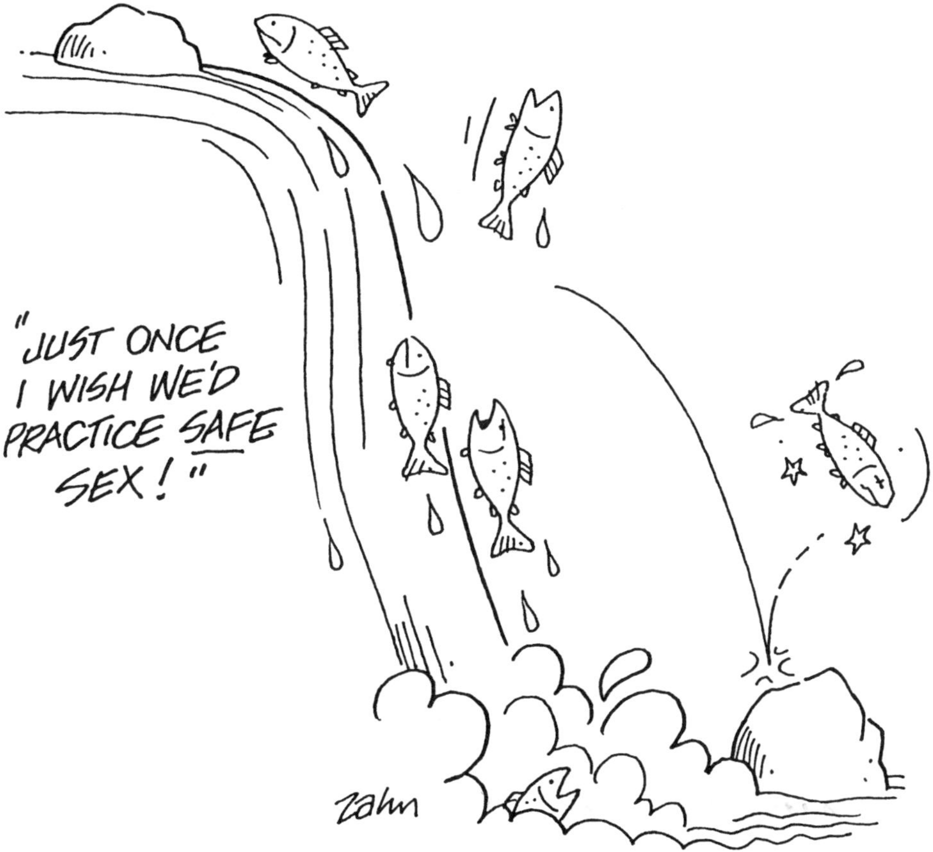
"JUST ONCE I WISH WE'D PRACTICE SAFE SEX!"
Zahn

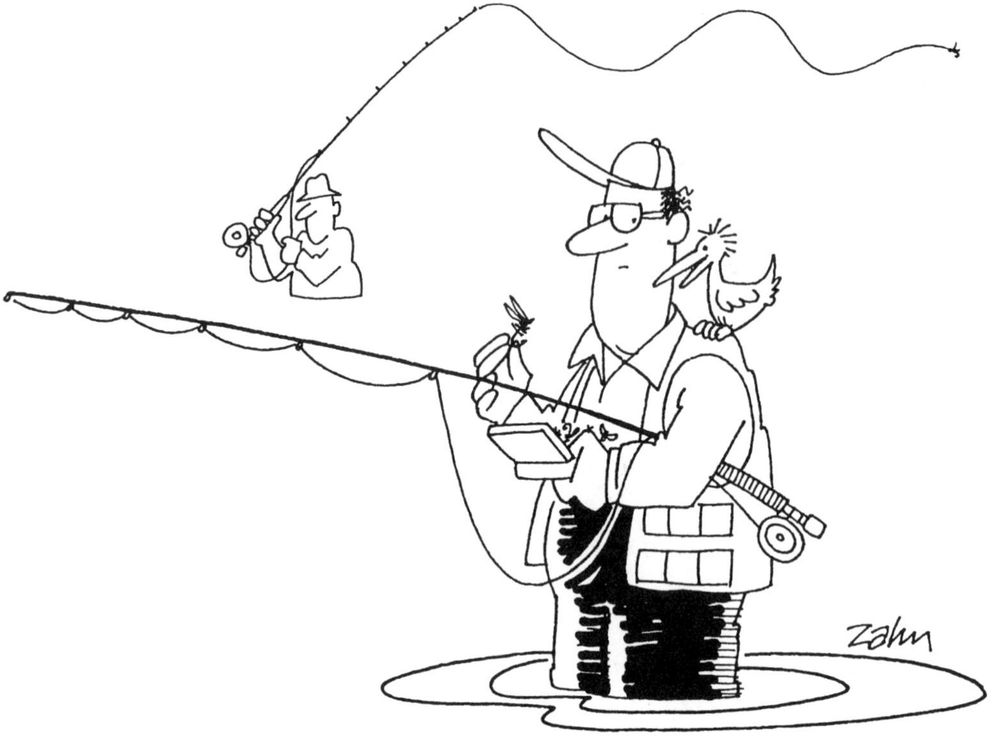
Zahn

"TRY SOMETHING PURPLE."

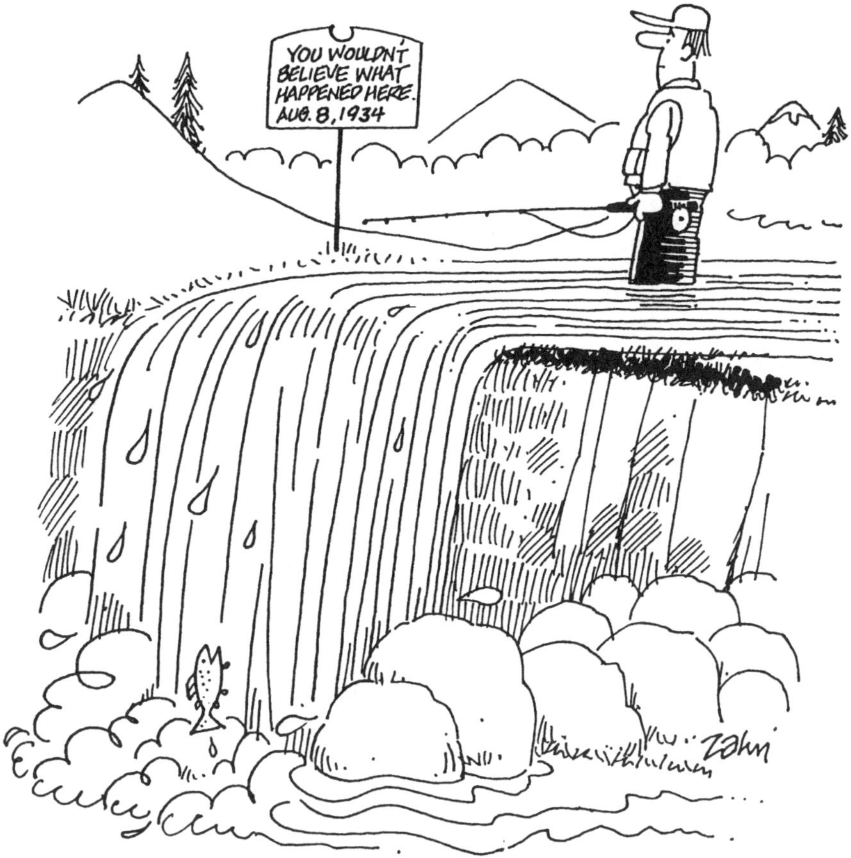
YOU WOULDN'T BELIEVE WHAT HAPPENED HERE. AUG. 8, 1934
Zahn

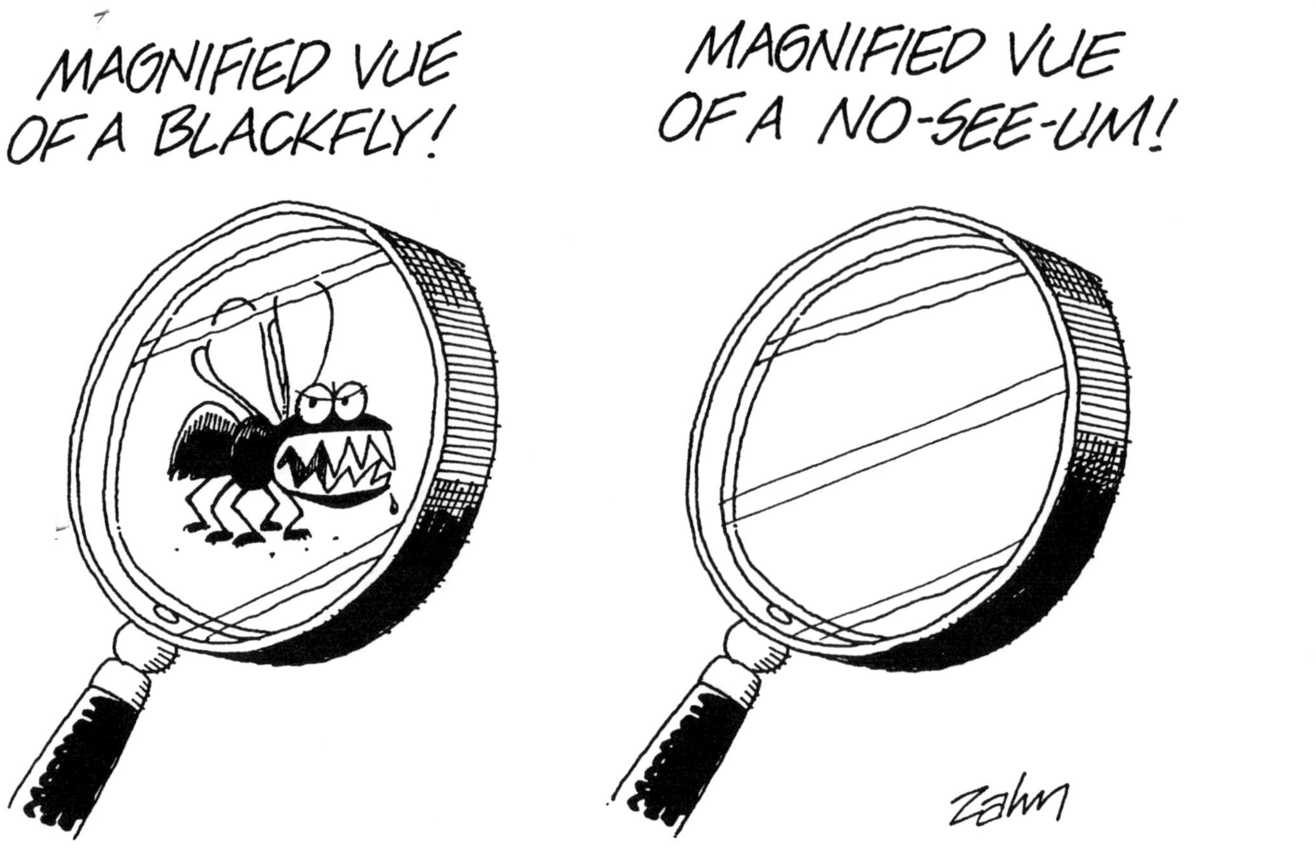
MAGNIFIED VUE OF A BLACKFLY!
MAGNIFIED VUE OF A NO-SEE-UM!
Zahn

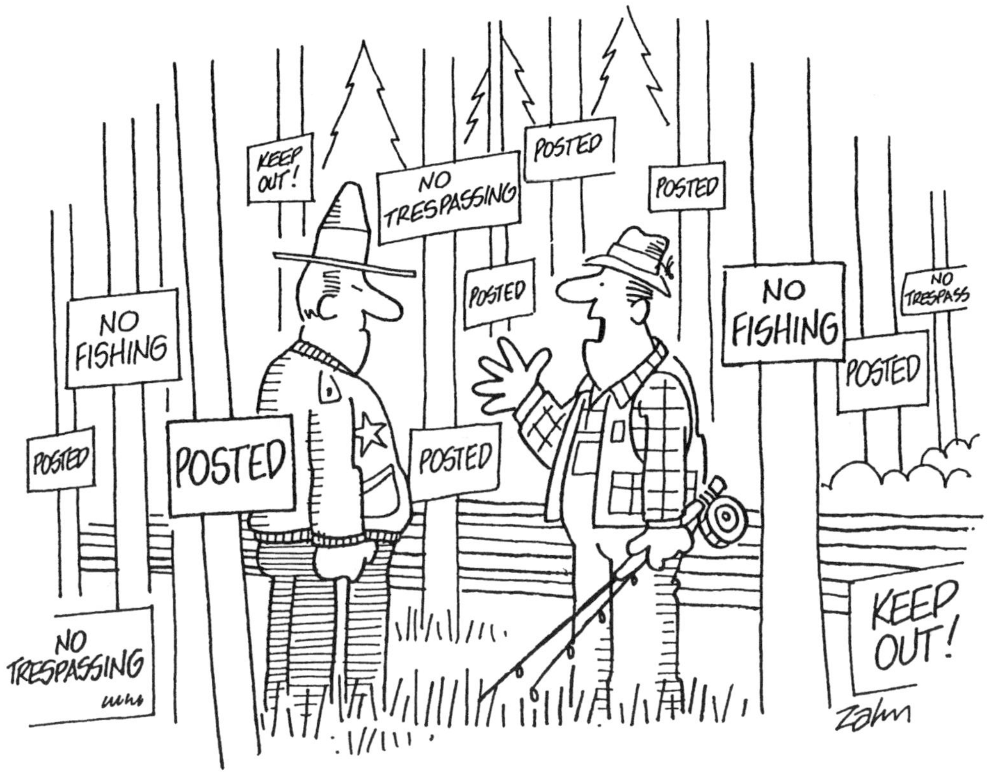
KEEP OUT!
NO TRESPASSING
POSTED
POSTED
POSTED
NO FISHING
NO TRESPASS
NO FISHING
POSTED
POSTED
POSTED
POSTED
NO TRESPASSING
KEEP OUT!
Zahn

"HONEST! I DIDN'T SEE THE SIGNS!"

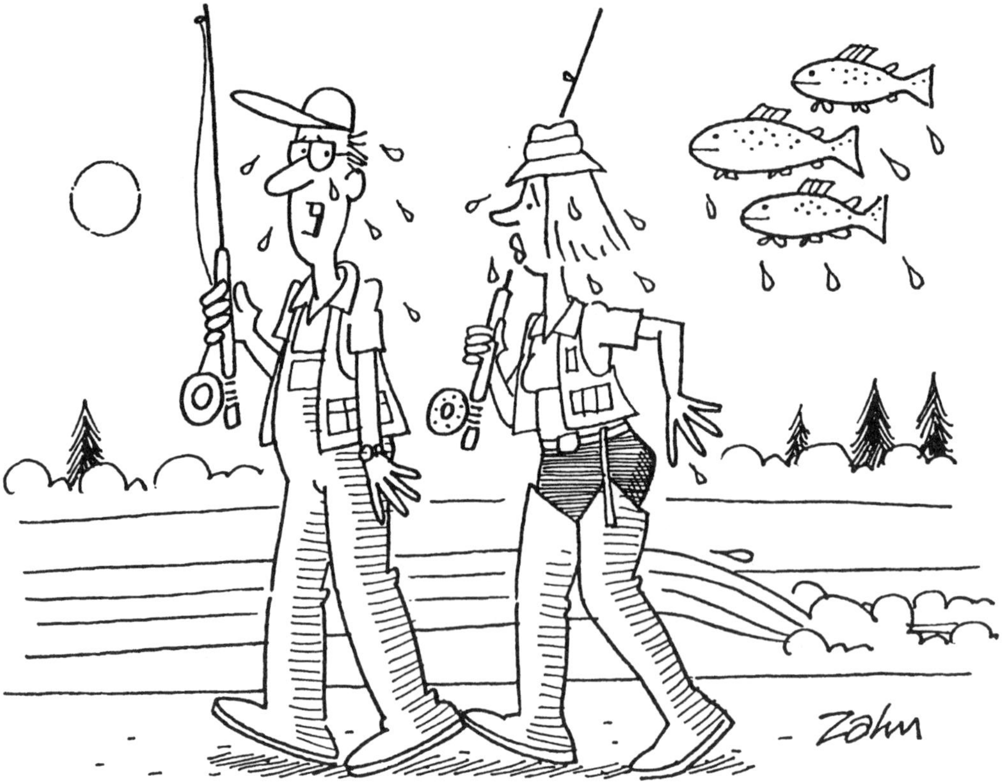
Zahn

"IS IT HUMID TODAY OR WHAT?"

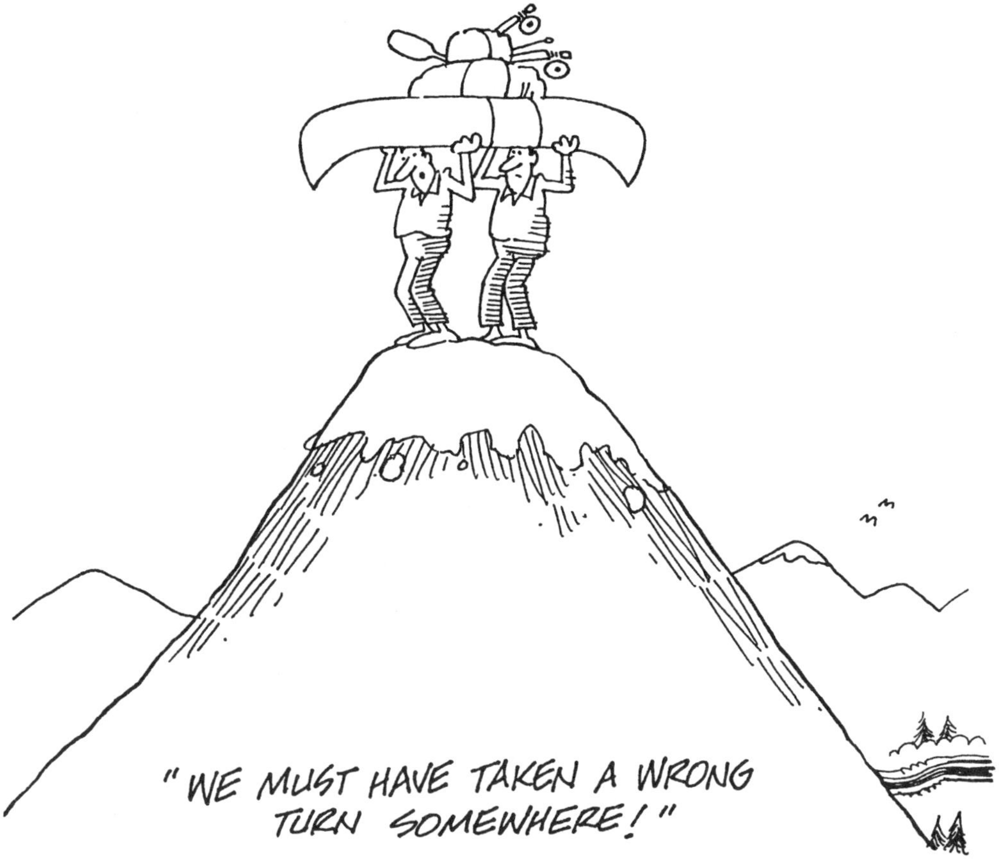
"WE MUST HAVE TAKEN A WRONG TURN SOMEWHERE!"

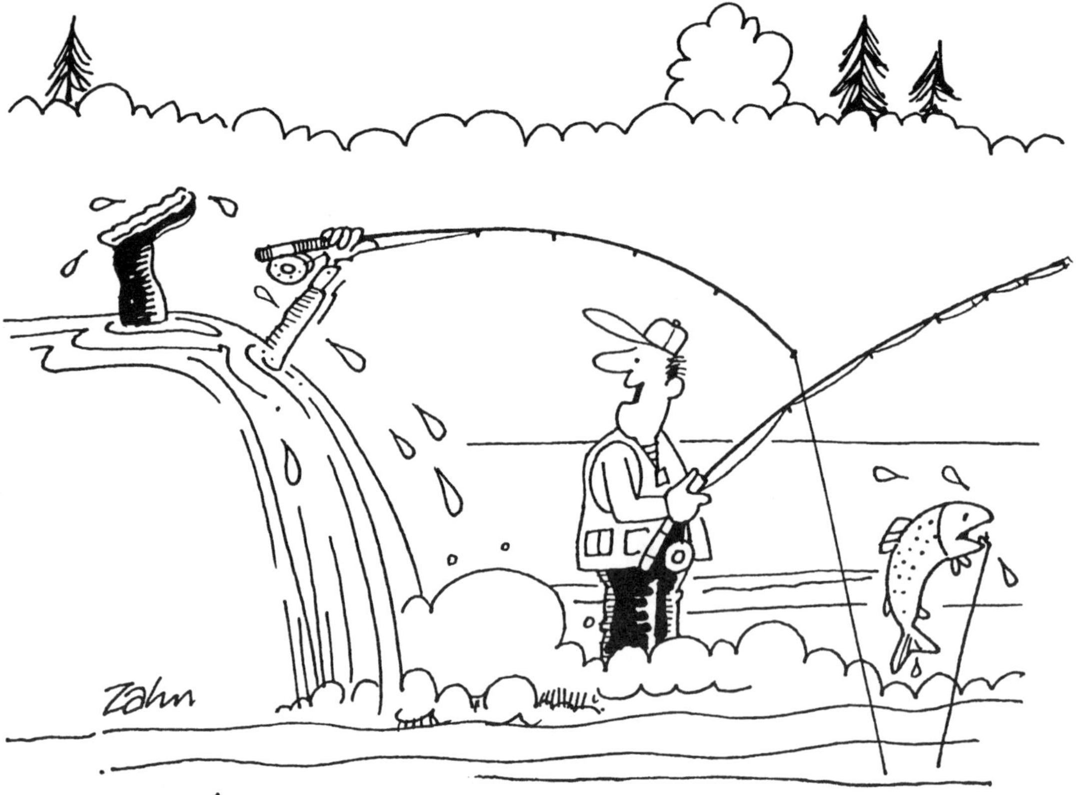
Zahn

"DON'T GIVE HIM ANY SLACK!"

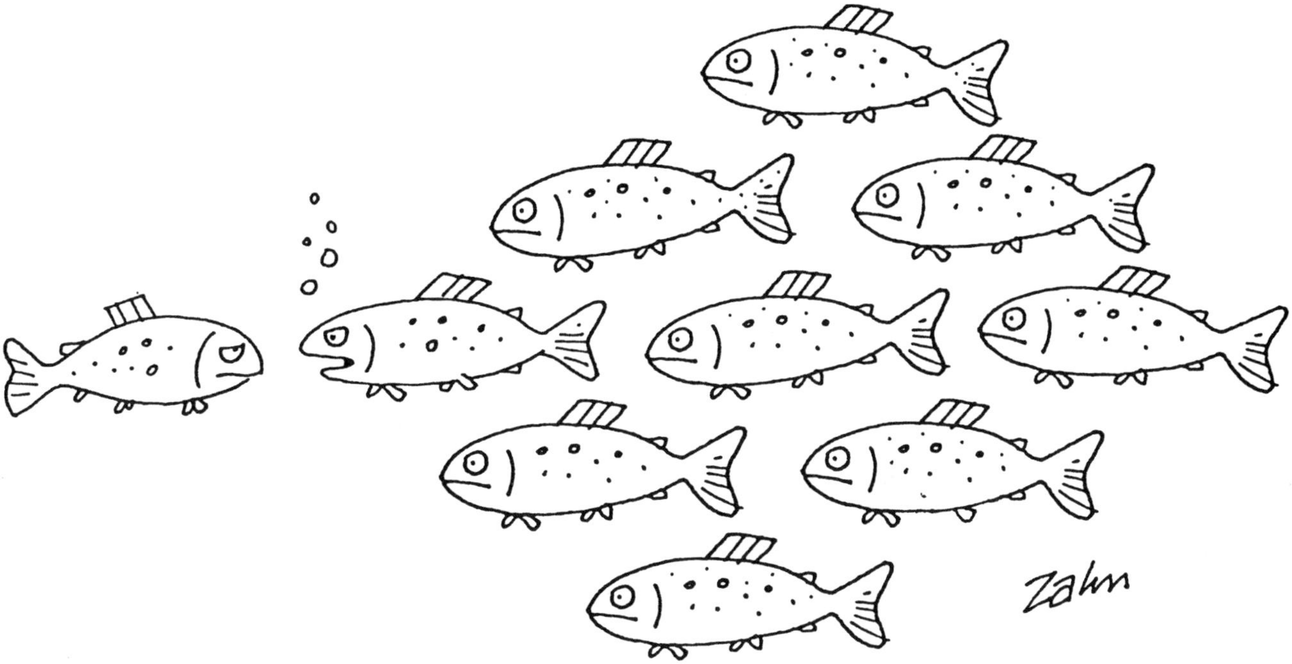
Zahn

"DON'T BE A FOOL—STAY IN SCHOOL!"

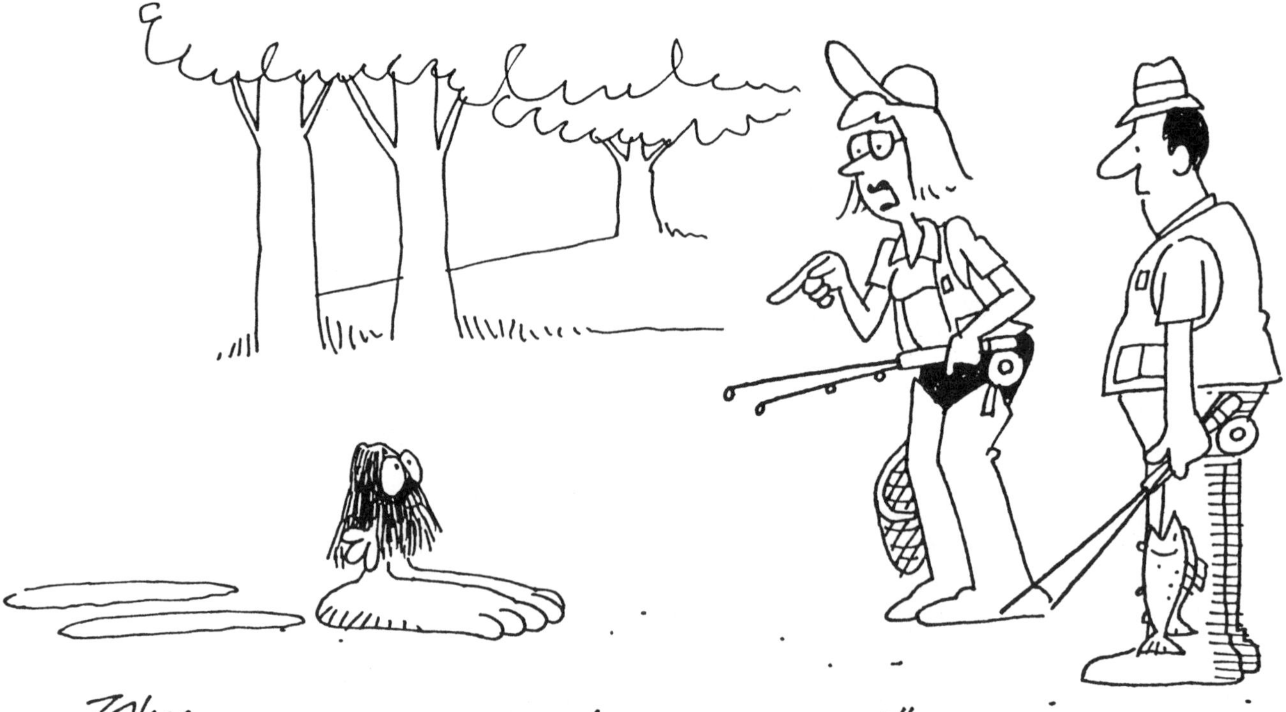

Zahn

"THAT'S BIGFOOT!?"

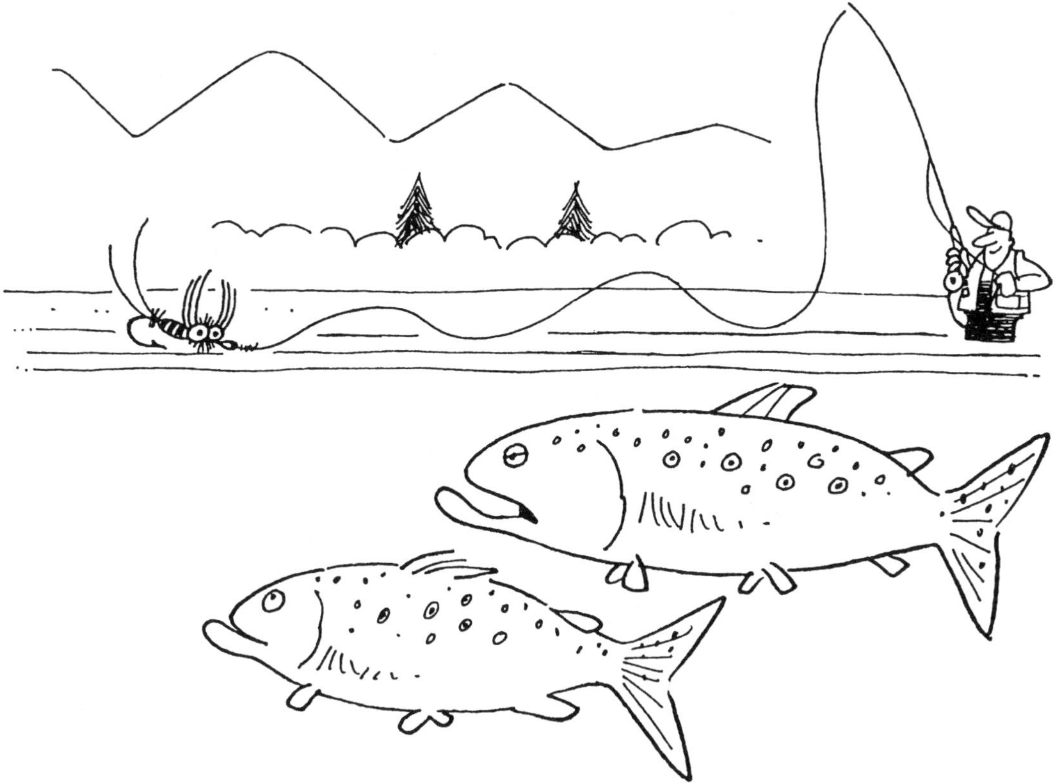

"I CONSIDER THAT AN INSULT TO MY INTELLIGENCE!"

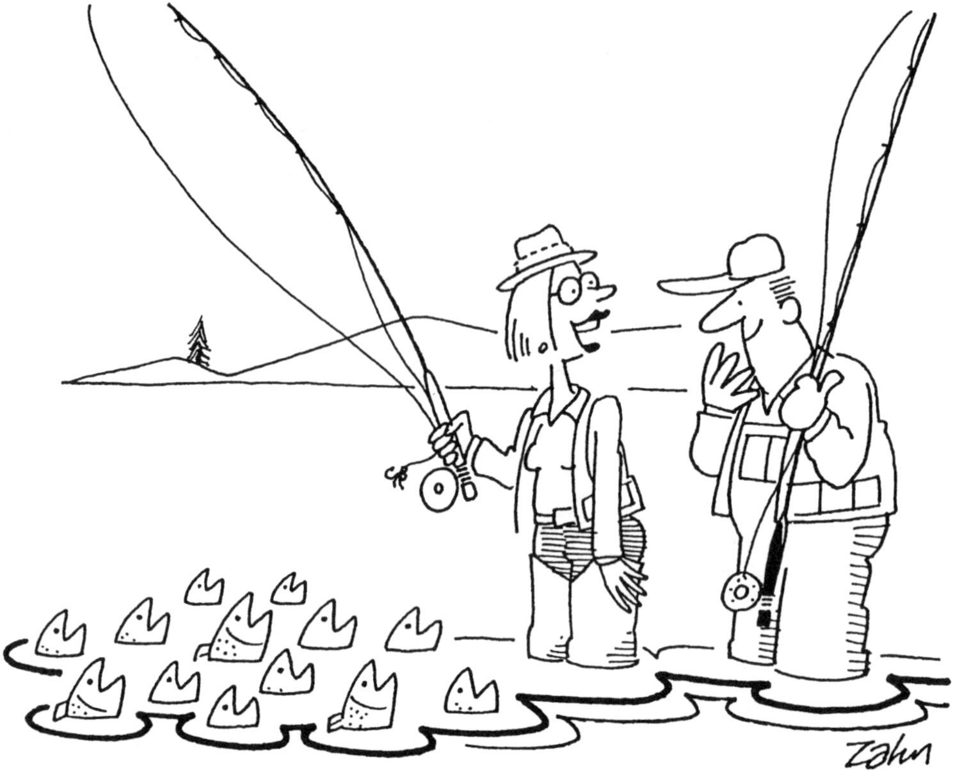
Zahn

"I THINK WE'RE REALLY GOING TO CATCH THEM THIS MORNING!"

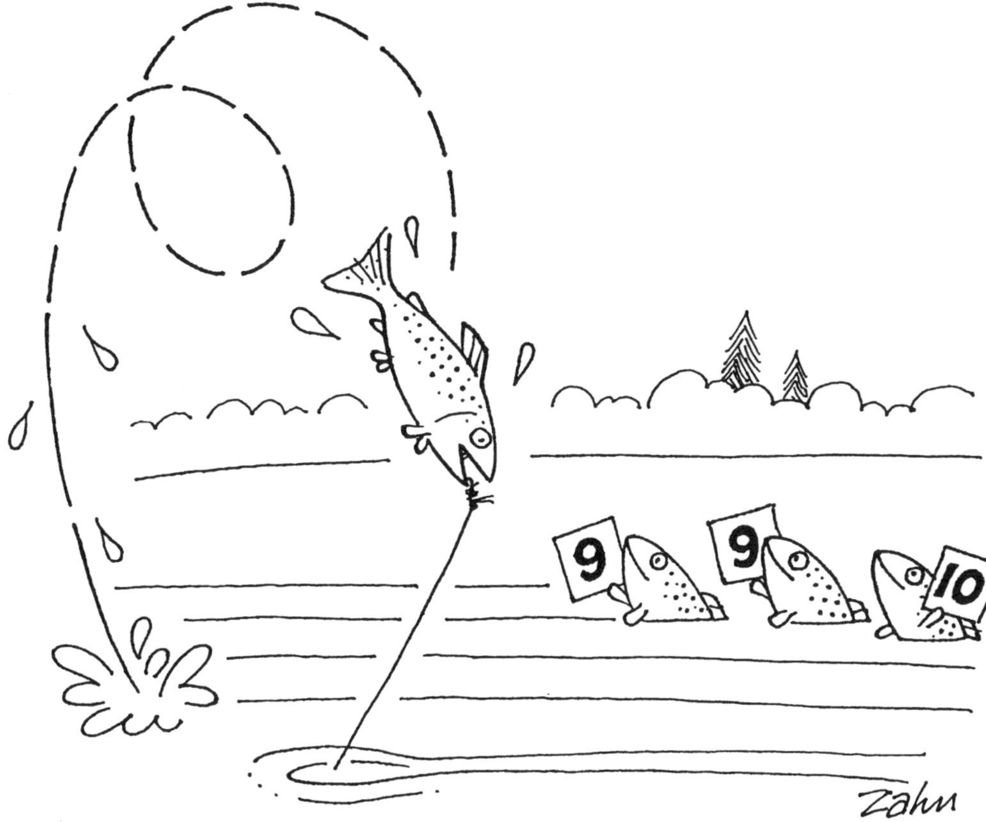
9
9
10
Zahn

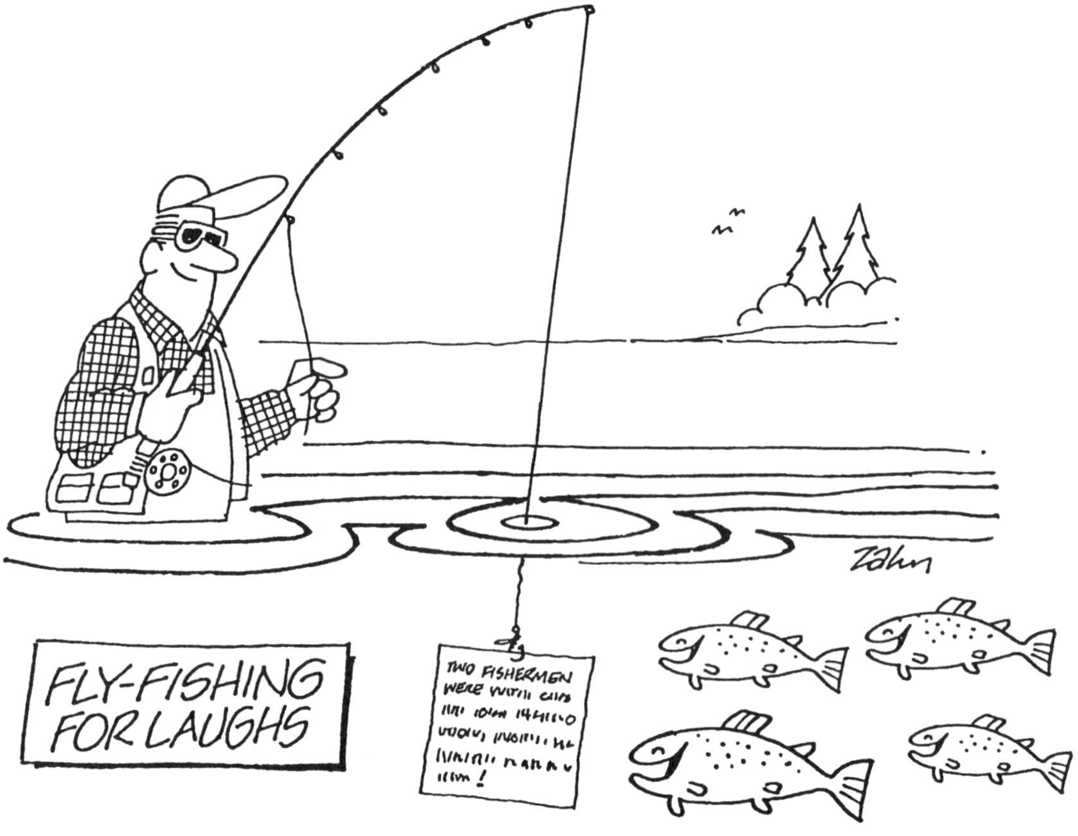
Zahn
FLY-FISHING FOR LAUGHS
TWO FISHERMEN
WERE

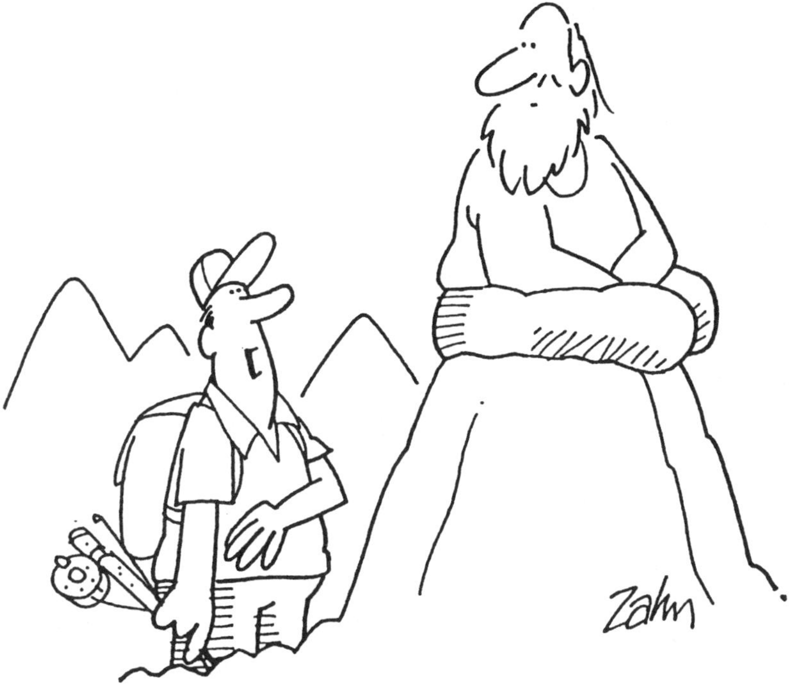
Zahn

"I DON'T CARE ABOUT THE MEANING OF LIFE...
I WANT TO KNOW HOW TO MATCH THE HATCH."

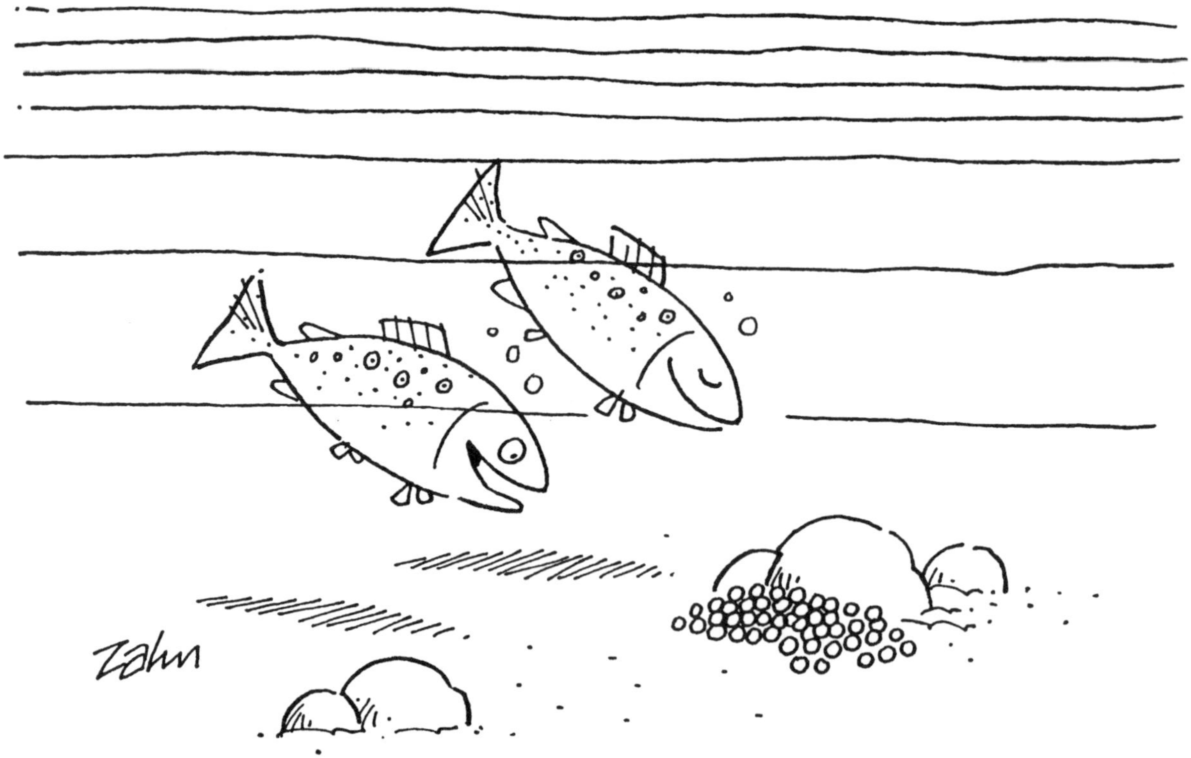
Zahn

"OH, YOUR EGGS ARE SOOOO CUTE!"

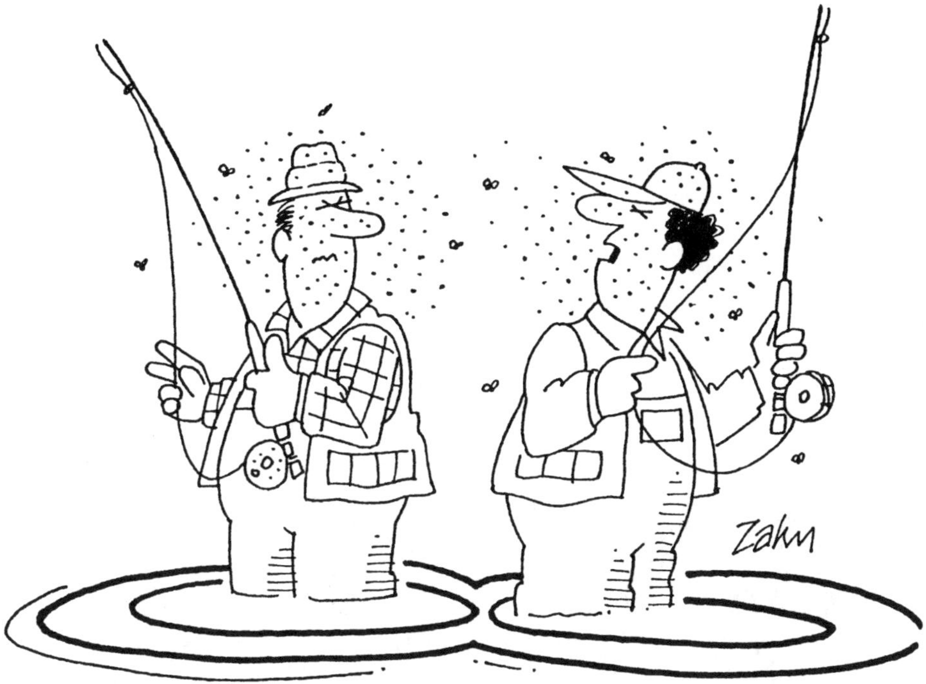
Zahn

"WHEN YOU SAID THEY WOULD BE BITING TODAY I THOUGHT YOU MEANT THE FISH!"

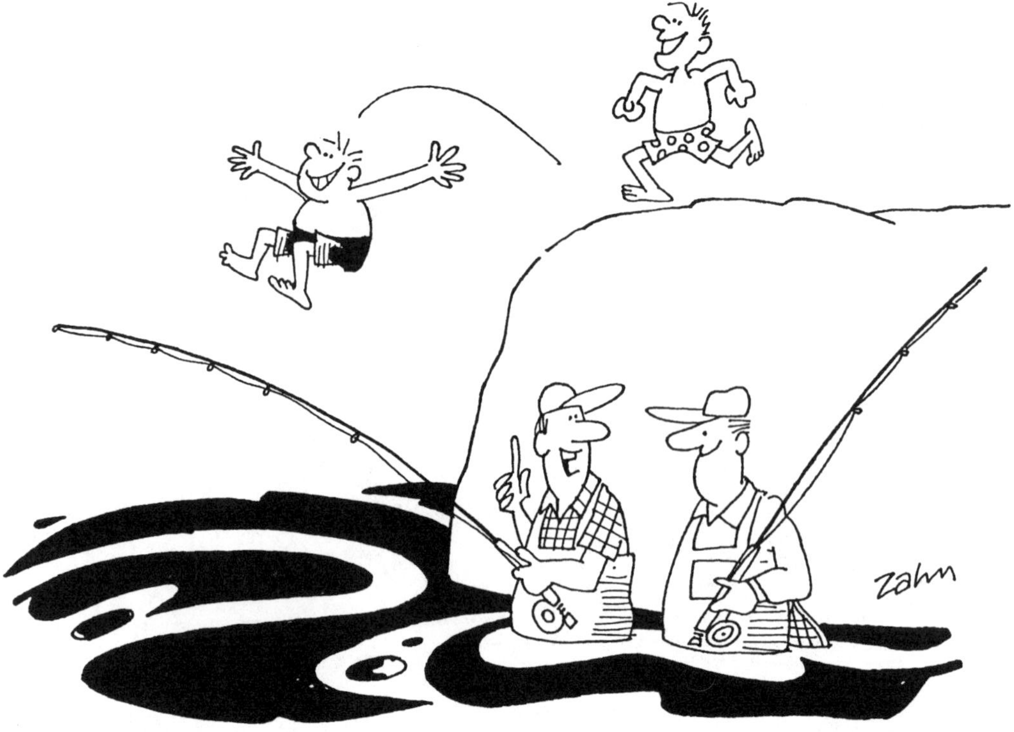
Zahn

"THIS IS A GREAT LOOKING POOL, DOUG. BE REAL QUIET SO WE DON'T SPOOK THE TROUT."

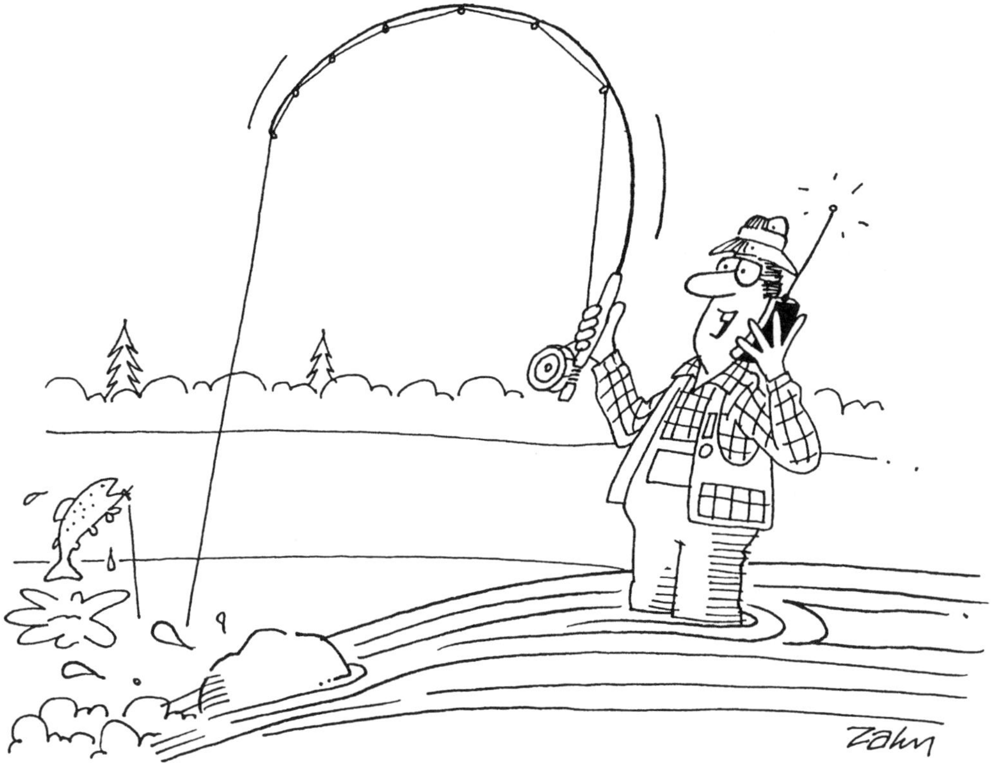
Zahn

"I CAN'T TALK TO YOU RIGHT NOW... I'LL CALL YOU BACK."

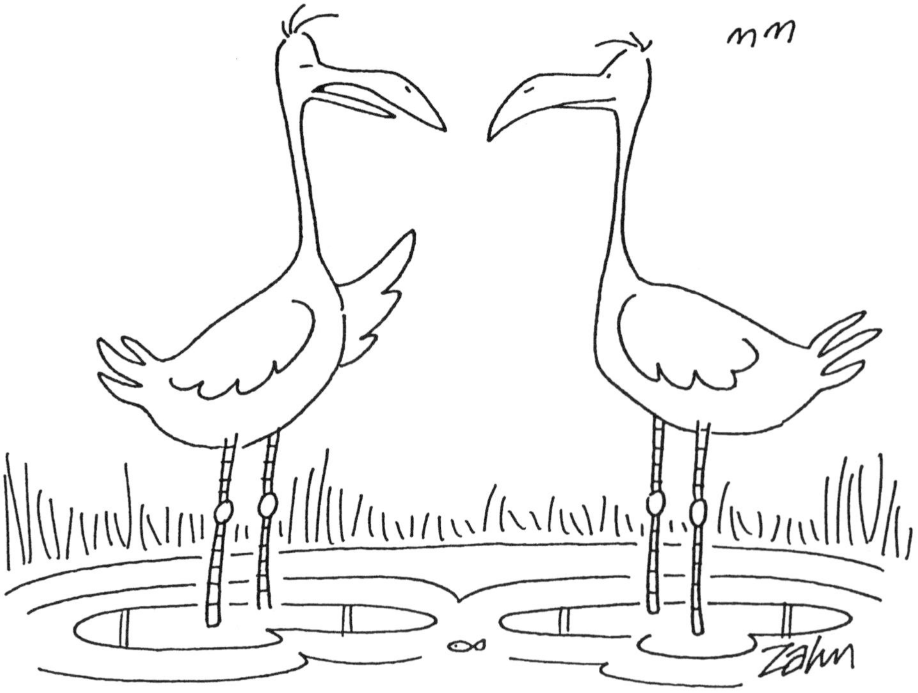

"REMEMBER, SON, A TROUT IN THE BEAK IS WORTH TWO IN THE STREAM."

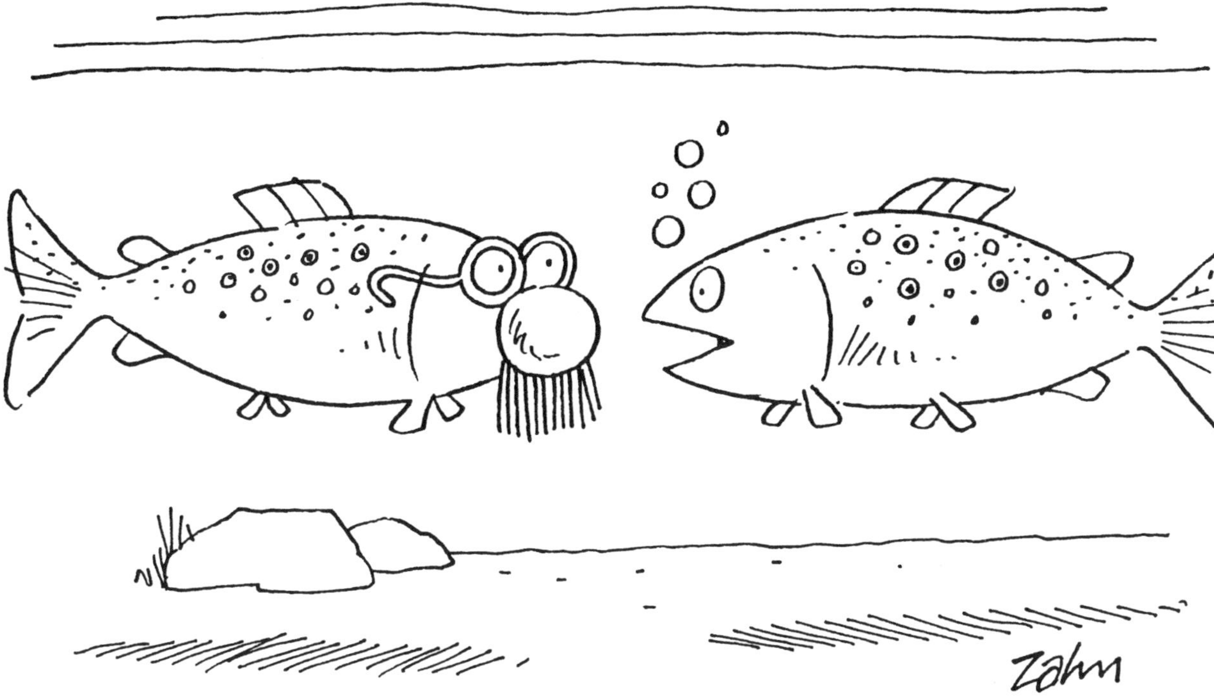
Zahn

"THE SEASON OPENS TOMORROW AND I DOUBT IF A DISGUISE WILL DO YOU MUCH GOOD IF YOU GET CAUGHT."

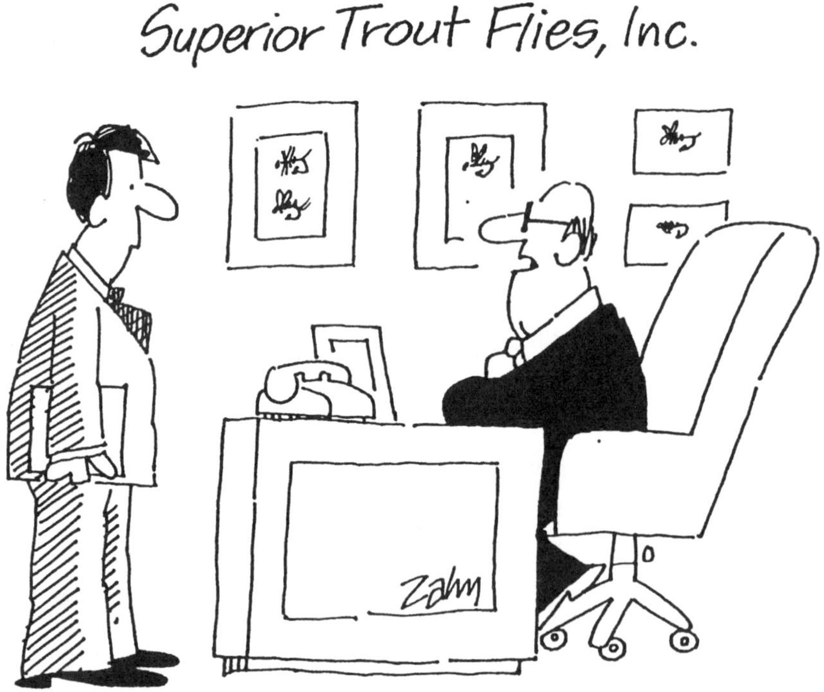
Superior Trout Flies, Inc.
Zahm

"IS THERE ANY TRUTH TO THE NASTY RUMOR THAT YOU HAVE BEEN KNOWN TO FISH WITH WORMS?"

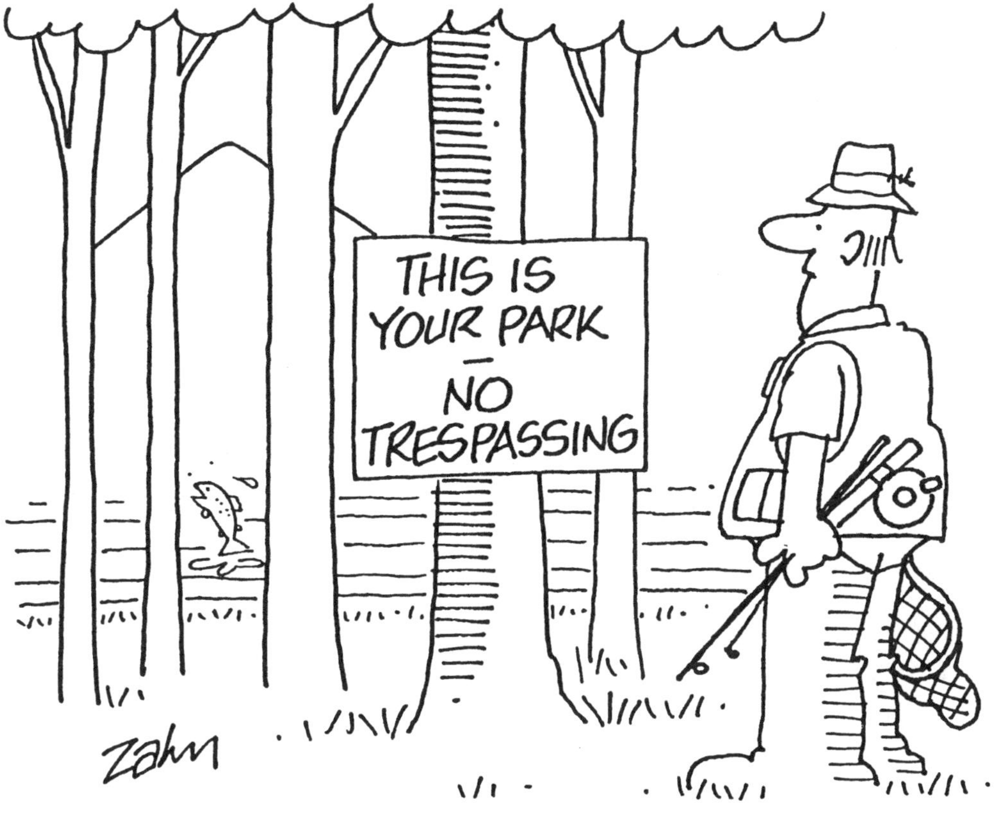
THIS IS
YOUR PARK
—
NO
TRESPASSING
Zahn

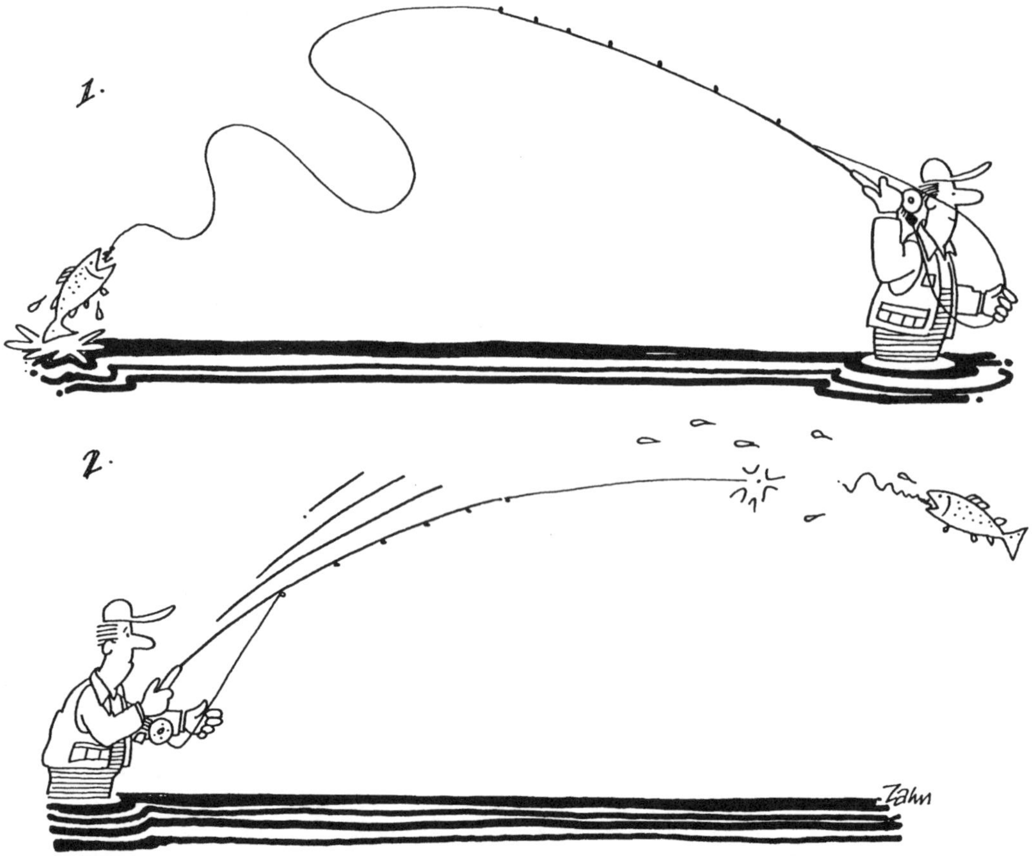
1.
2.
Zahn

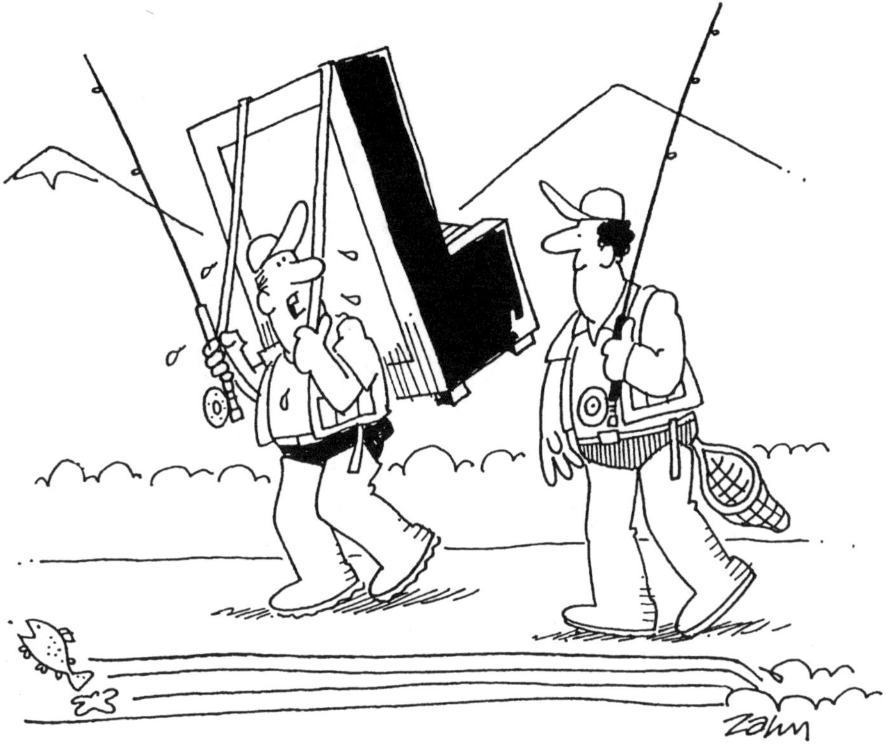
Zahn

"MY MOTHER WOULD BE REALLY MAD AT ME IF I DIDN'T PRACTICE THE PIANO EVERY DAY!"

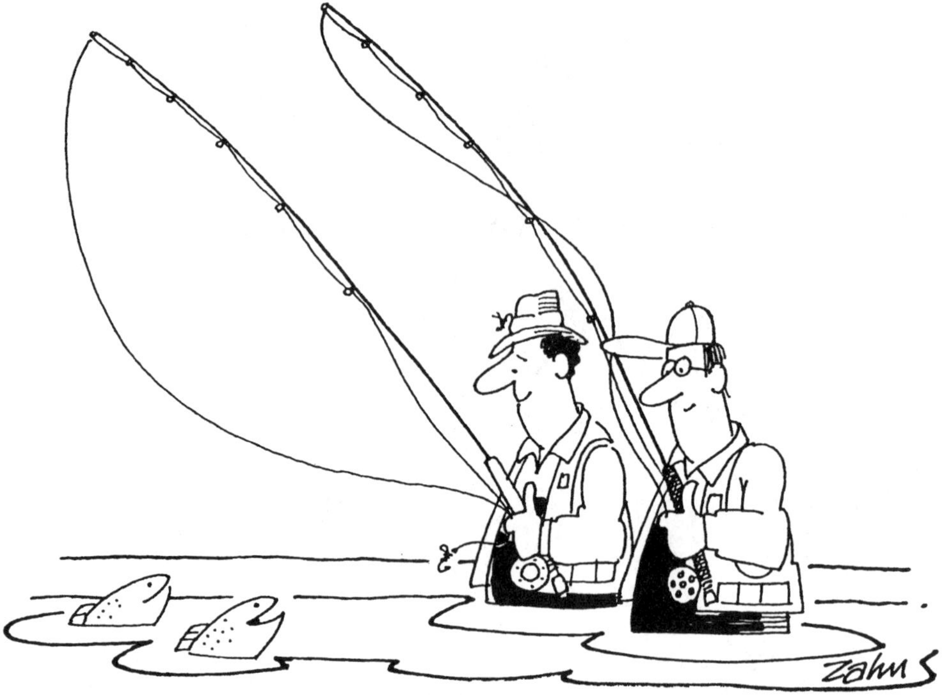

"WE DON'T MIND PUTTING ON AN AERIAL SHOW FOR YOU GUYS AS LONG AS YOU USE BARBLESS HOOKS AND PRACTICE CATCH AND RELEASE."

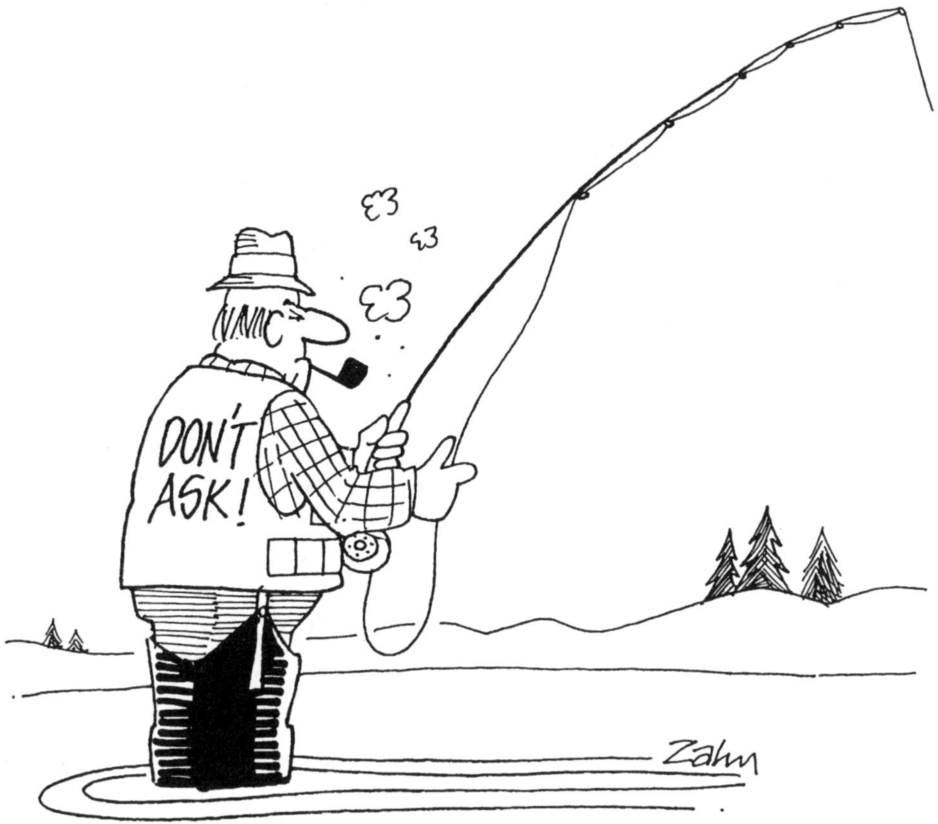
DON'T ASK!
Zahn

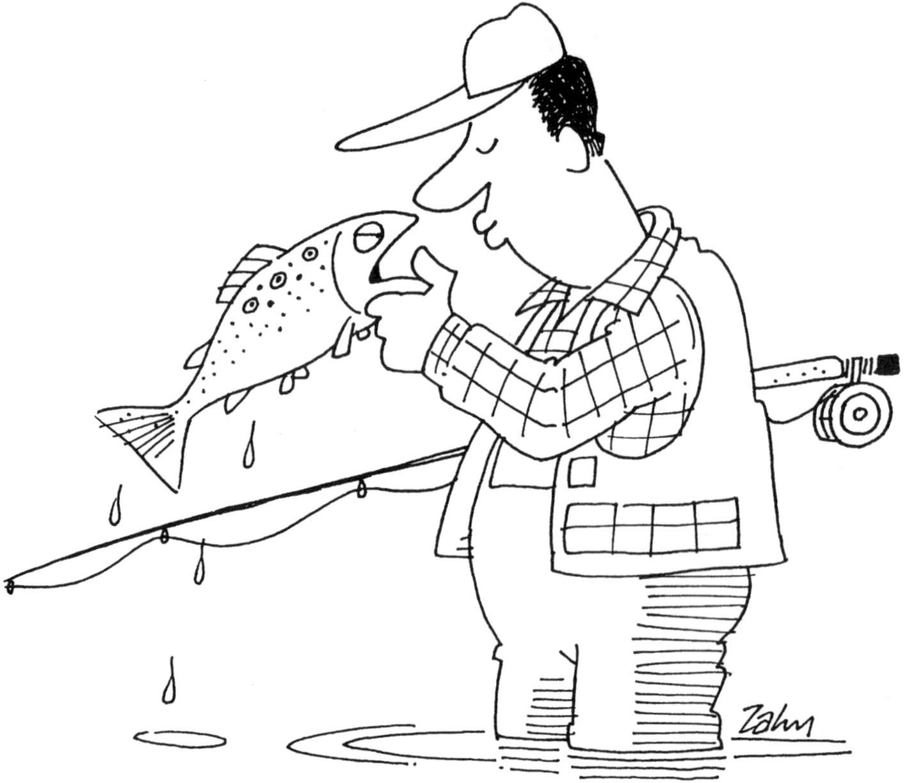
Zahn

"I APPRECIATE YOU RELEASING ME, BUT NO KISSES!"

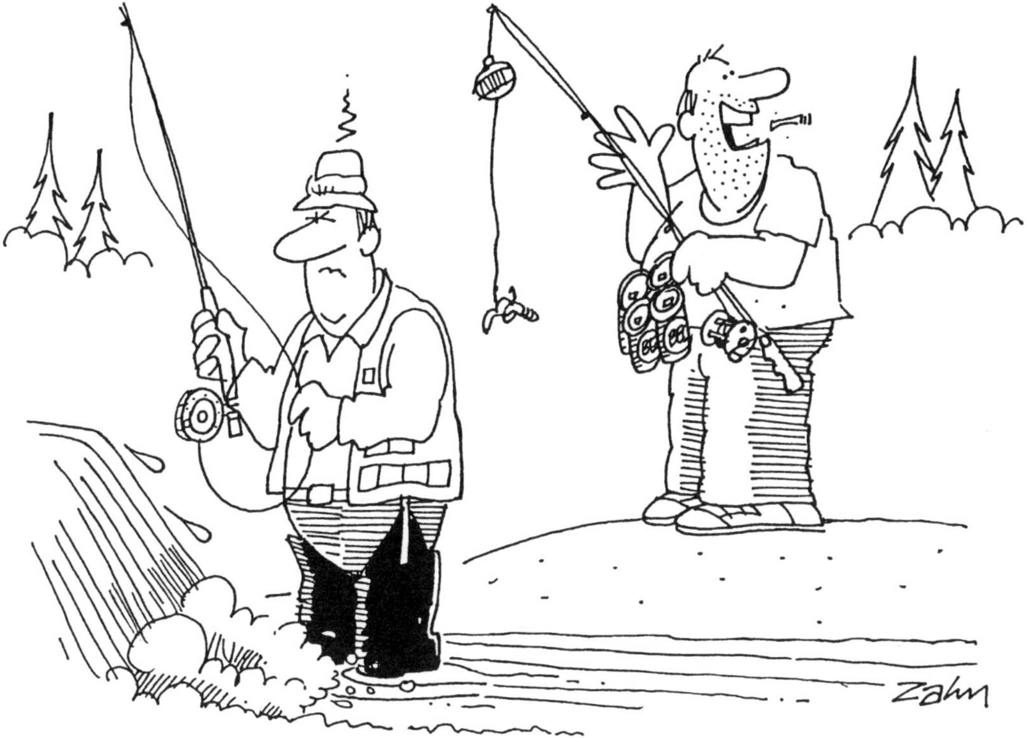
Zahn

"THIS LOOKS LIKE A GOOD SPOT, MOMMA. BRING GRANDMA AND THE KIDS!"

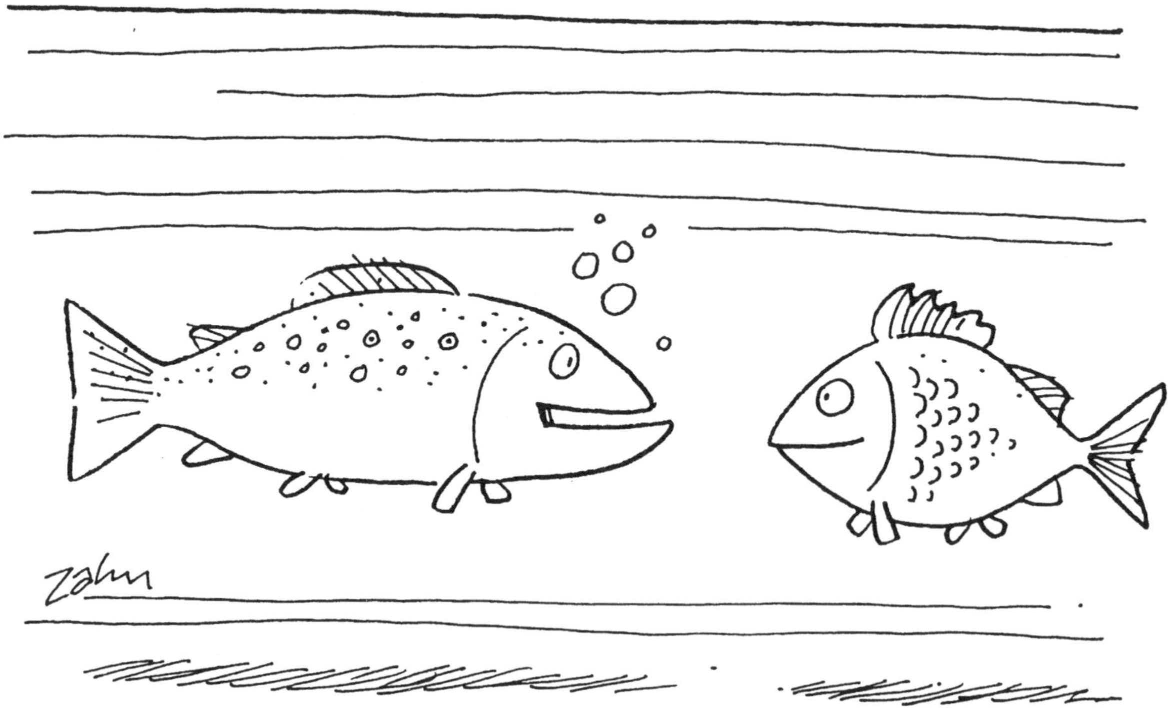
Zahn

"YOU'LL HAVE TO EXCUSE ME... I'M A SALMON AND I HAVE TO RUN."

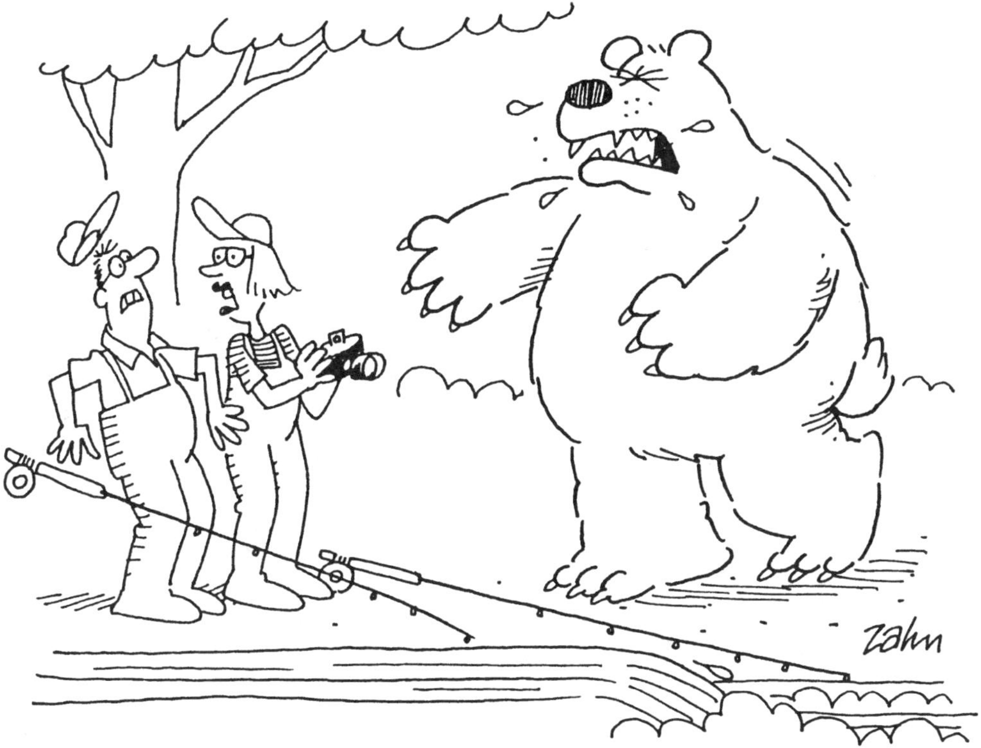
Zahn

"WOULDN'T YOU KNOW IT! I'M OUT OF FILM!"

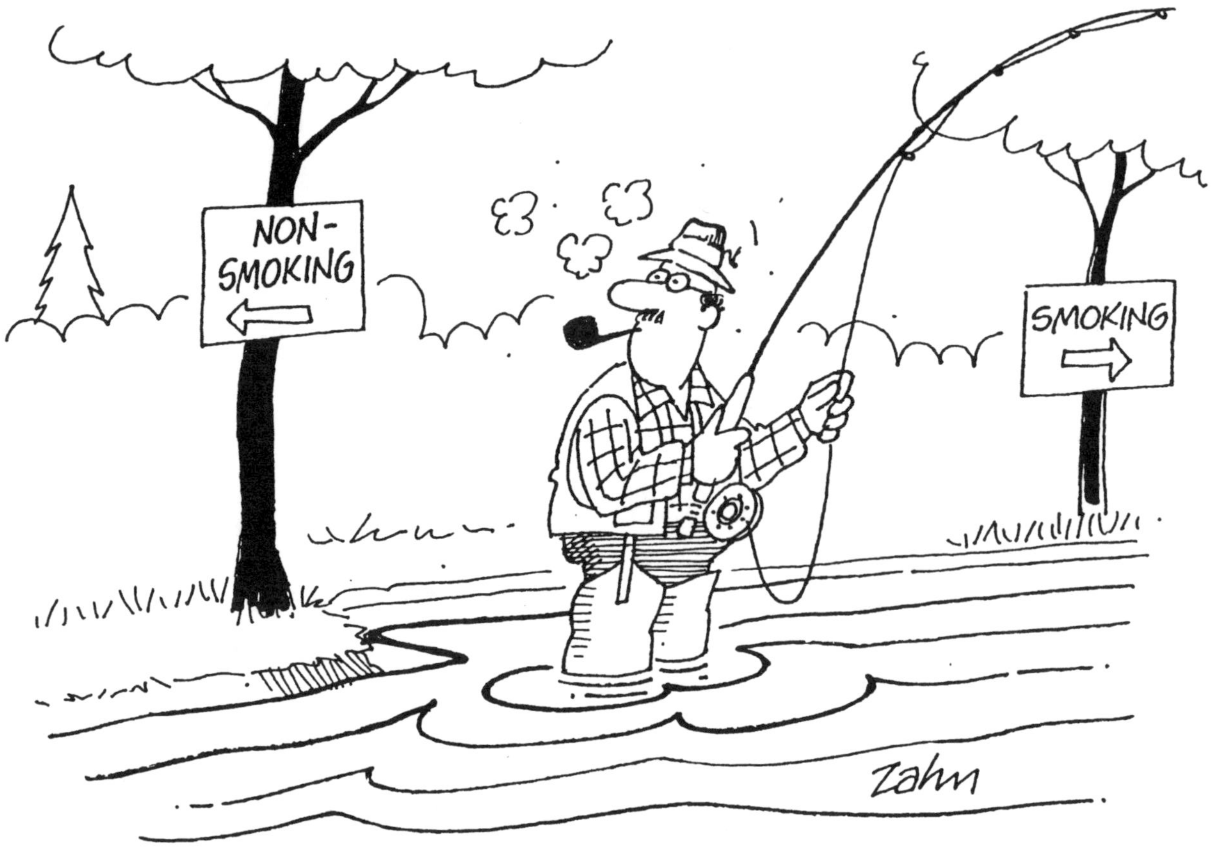
NON-
SMOKING
SMOKING
Zahn

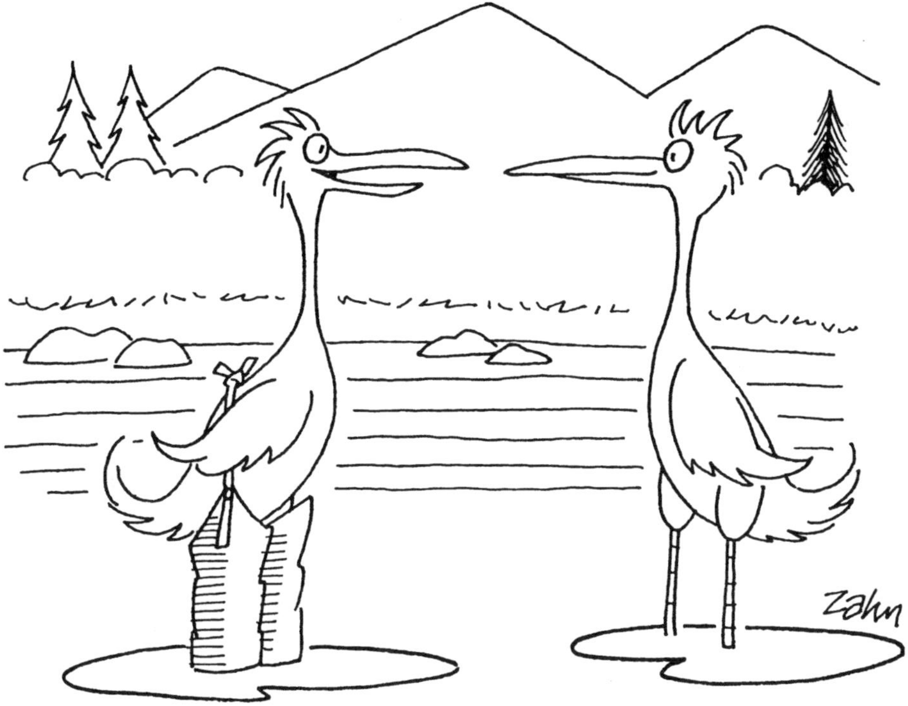
Zahn

"I FOUND THEM BESIDE THE STREAM. IT'S REALLY GREAT TO FISH WITH DRY FEET!"

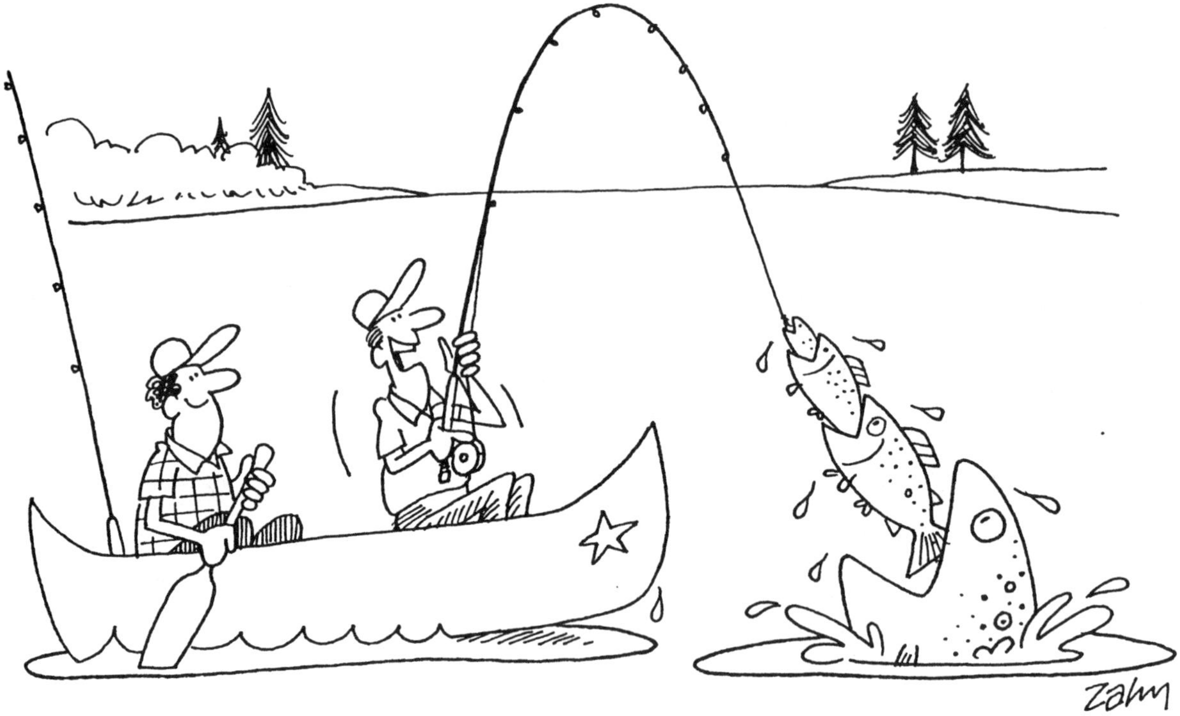
zahn

" YOU DREAM OF DAYS LIKE THIS ! "

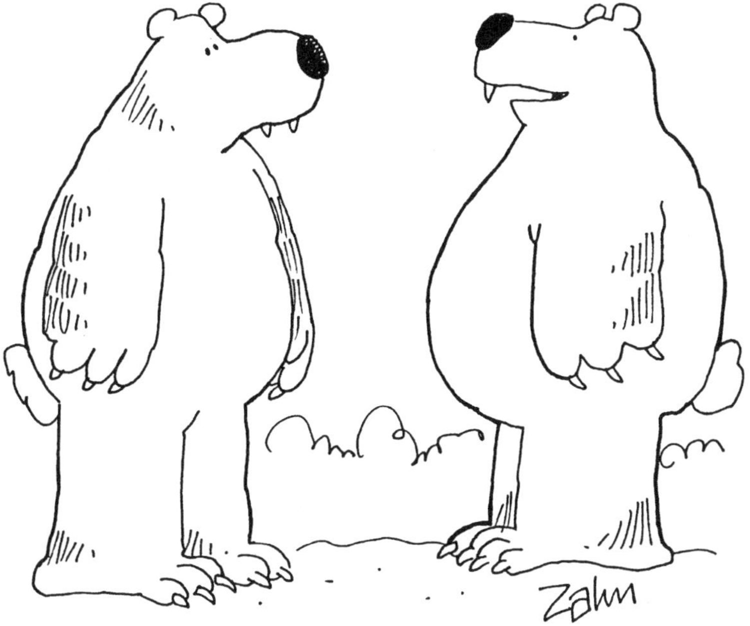
Zahn

"I HAD A GREAT DAY DOWN AT THE STREAM! I CAUGHT SIX SALMON AND SCARED THE PANTS OFF THREE FLY FISHERMEN!"

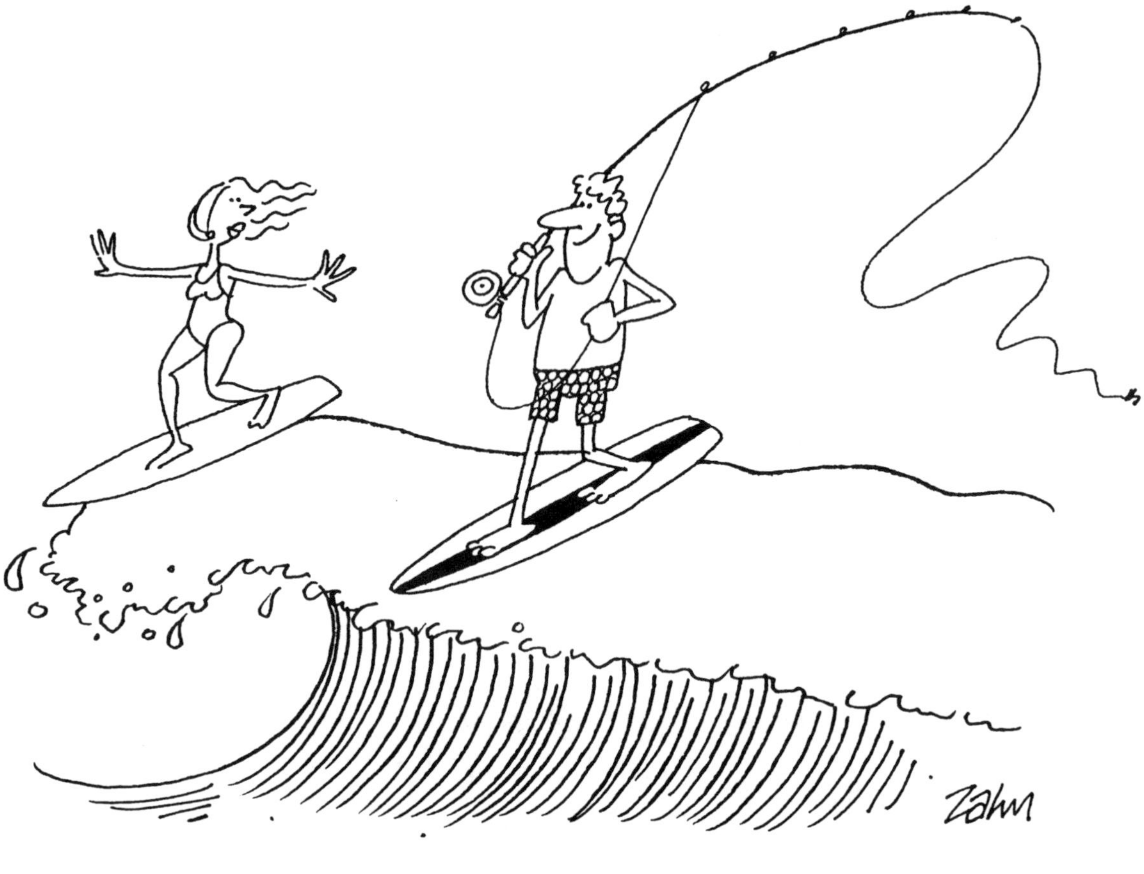
Zahn

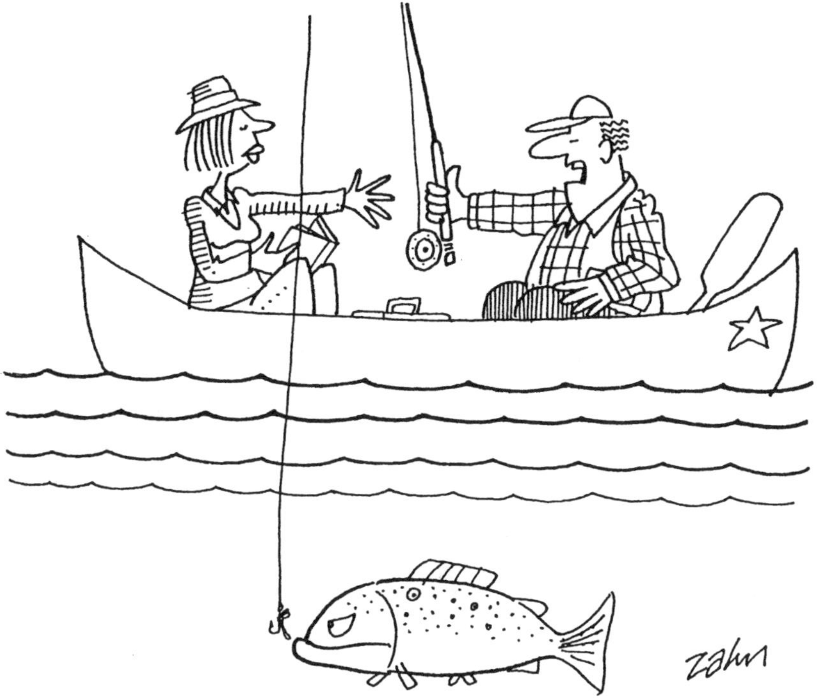
zahn

"I CAN'T BELIEVE I'VE BEEN CASTING ALL MORNING WITHOUT A SINGLE STRIKE! HERE, HOLD MY ROD FOR A COUPLE OF MINUTES WHILE I REST MY ARM."

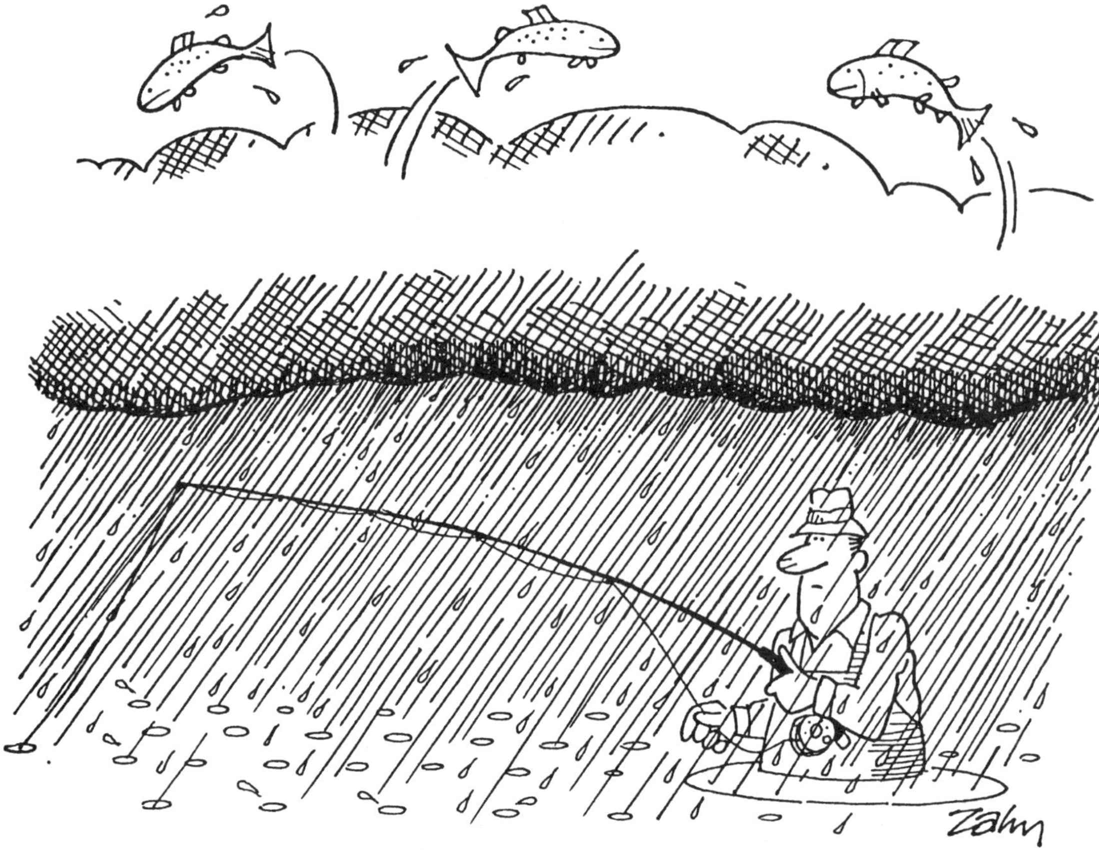
Zahn

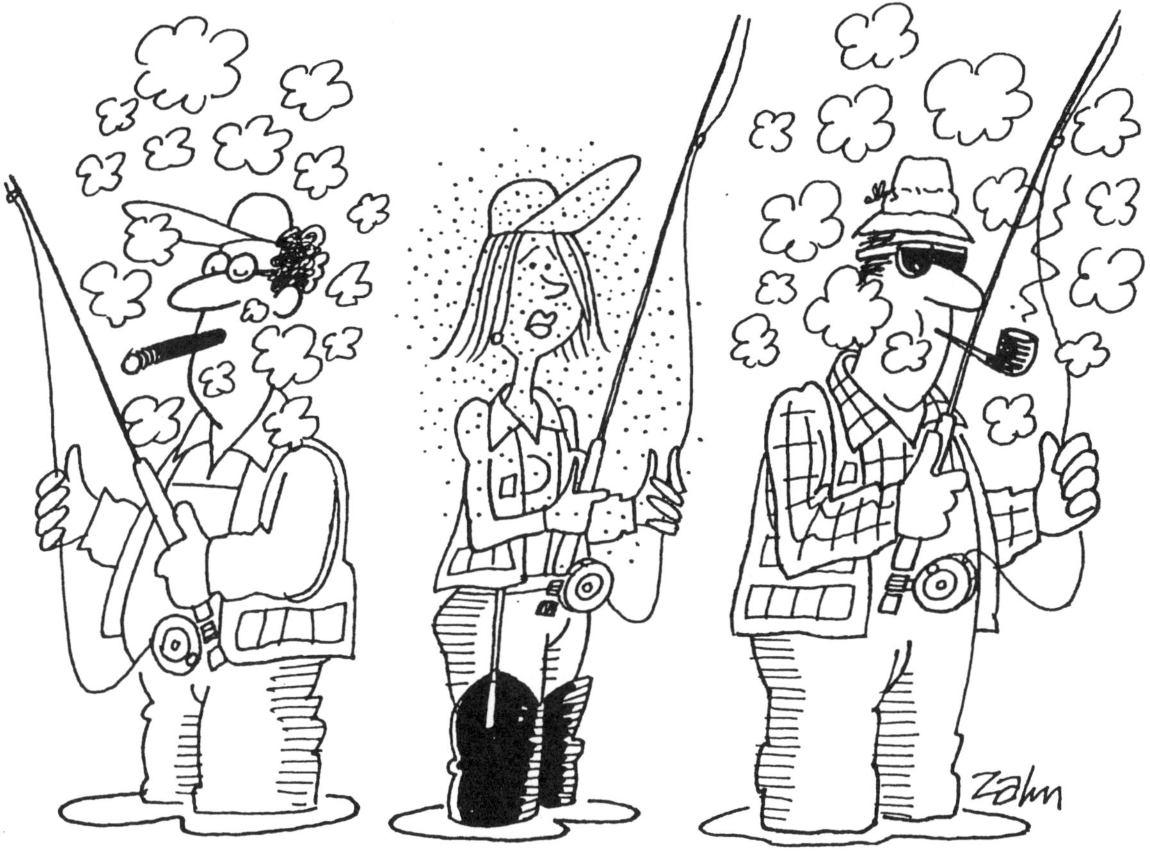
Zahn

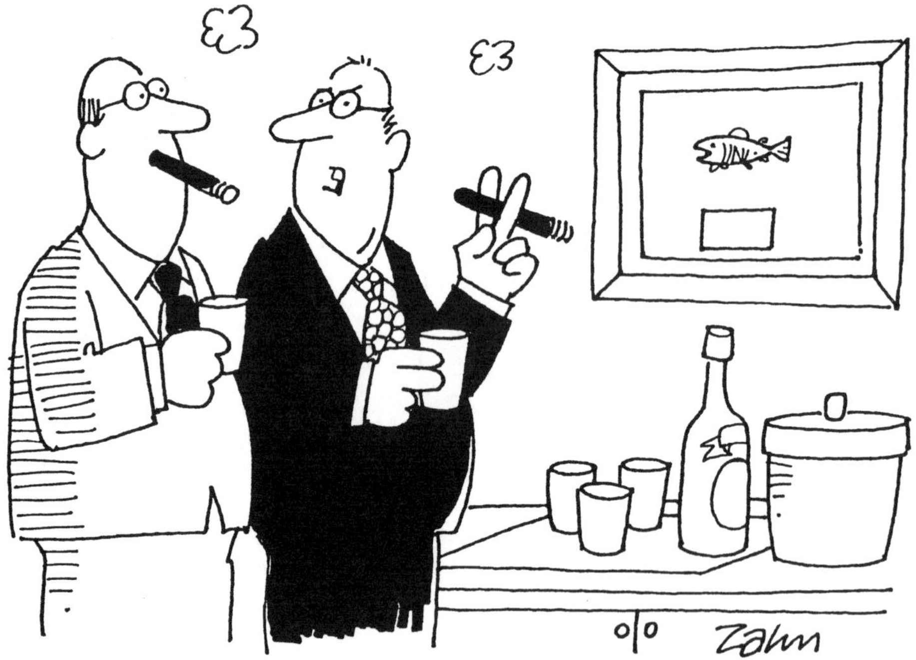
Zahn

"I SPENT $1500 ON NEW EQUIPMENT, $4000 ON THE TRIP AND ALL I CAUGHT WAS THAT CREEK CHUB... ...YOU'RE DARN RIGHT I HAD HIM MOUNTED!"

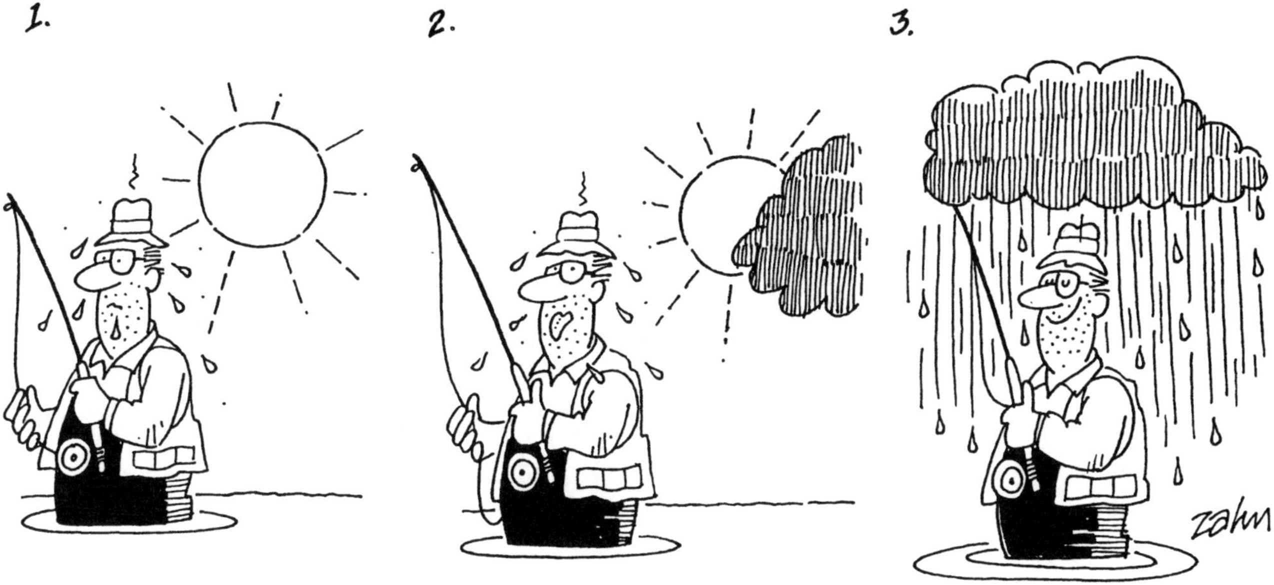
1.
2.
3.
zahn

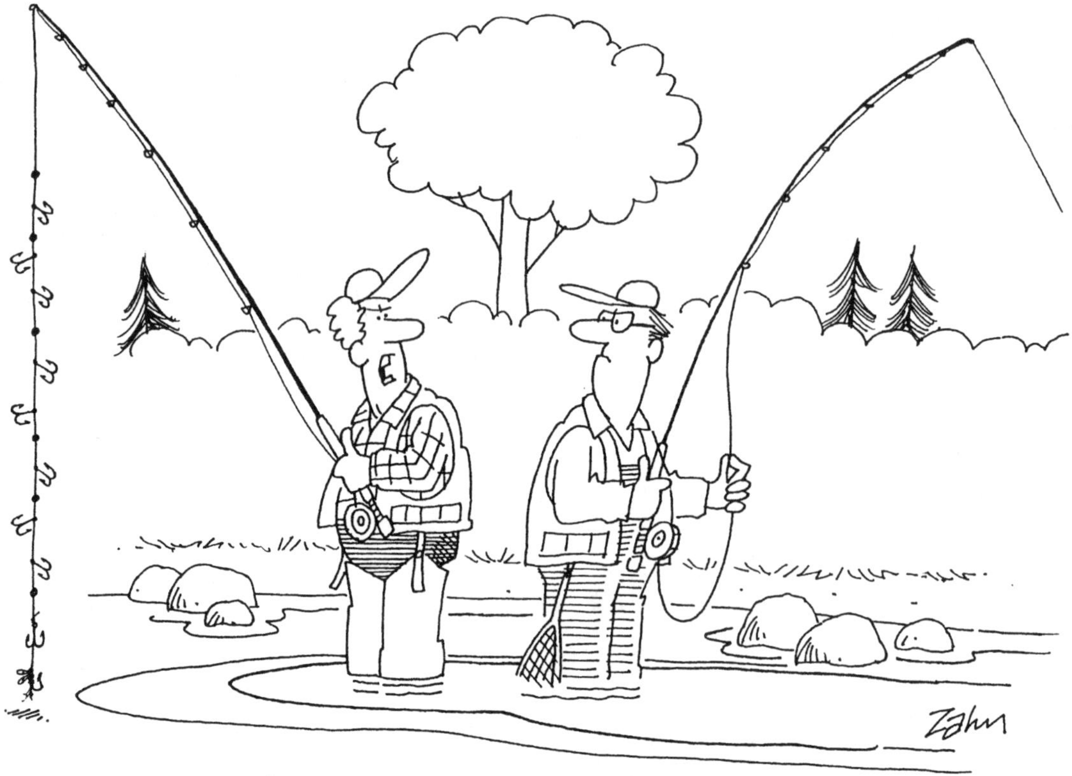
Zahn

"SNAGGING! WHO'S SNAGGING?"

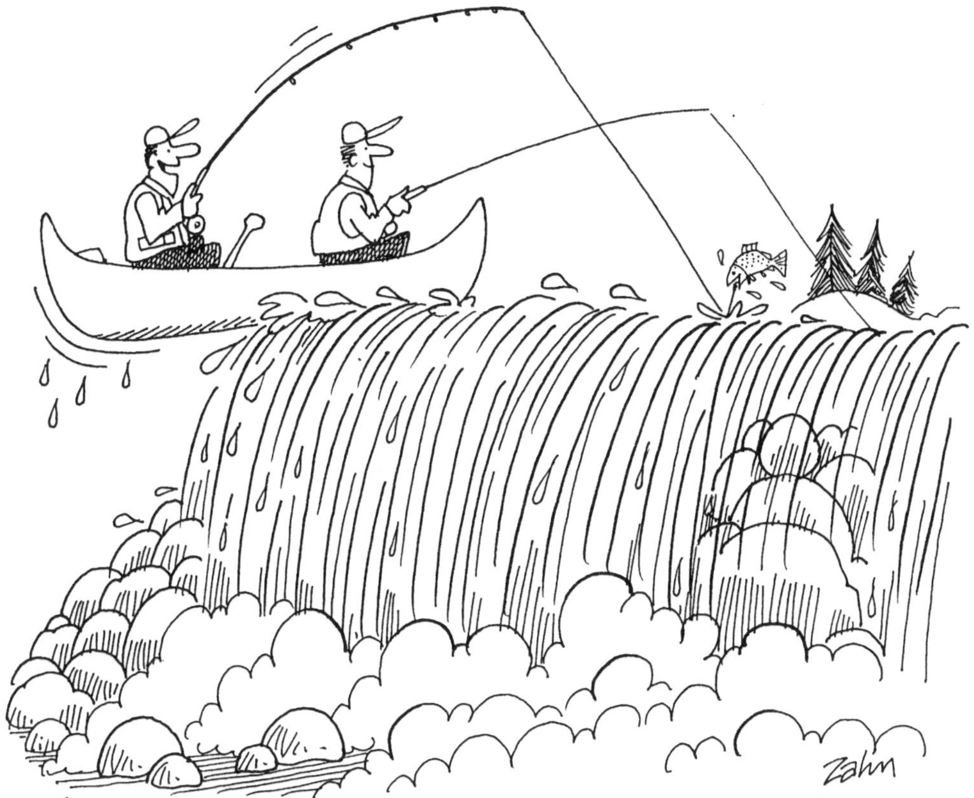
Zahn

"IT DOESN'T GET ANY BETTER THAN THIS, RALPH!"

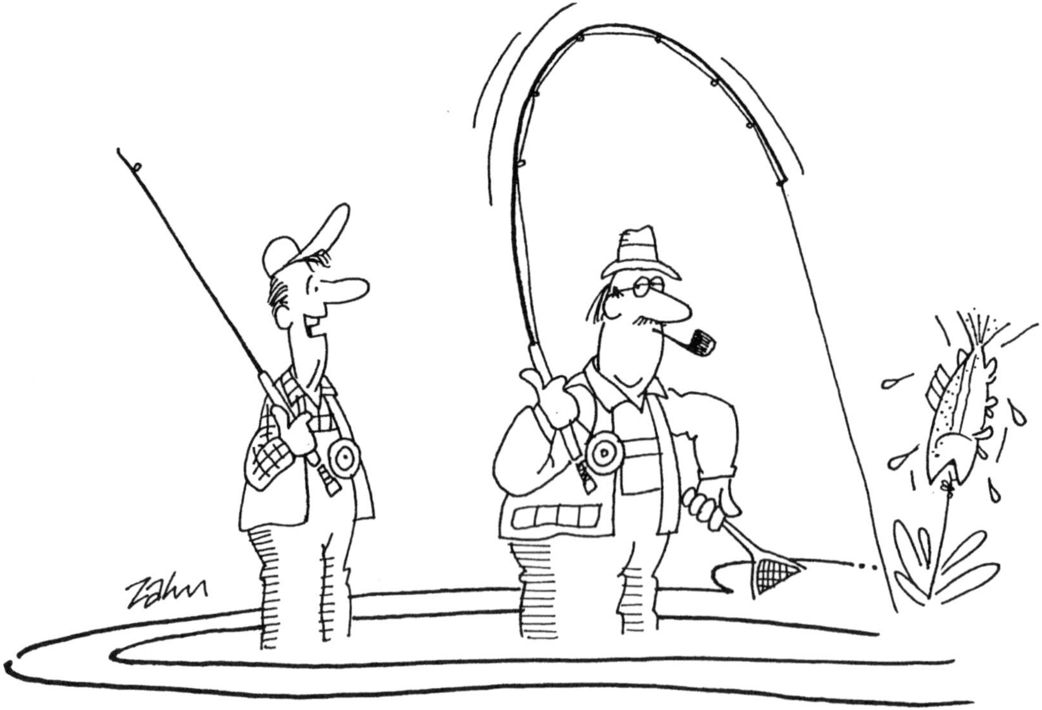
Zahn

"I'VE BEEN FISHING FOR STEELHEAD FOR 20 YEARS. I'VE NEVER ACTUALLY CAUGHT ONE, BUT IF I DID I'D RELEASE HIM."

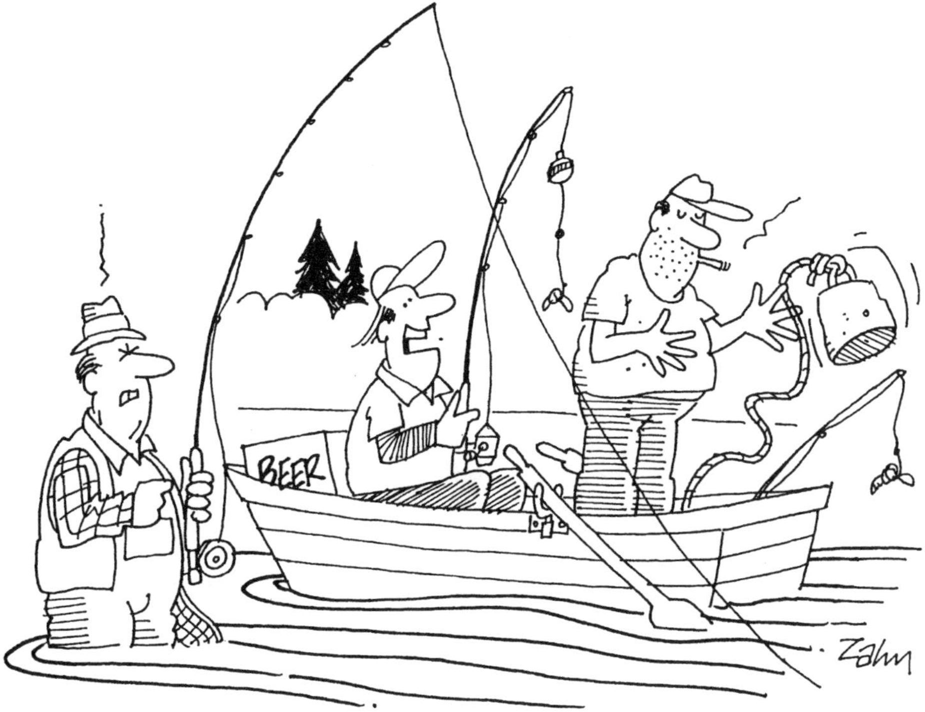

BEER
Zahn

"THIS LOOKS LIKE A GOOD SPOT, HARRY. THROW OUT THE ANCHOR!!"

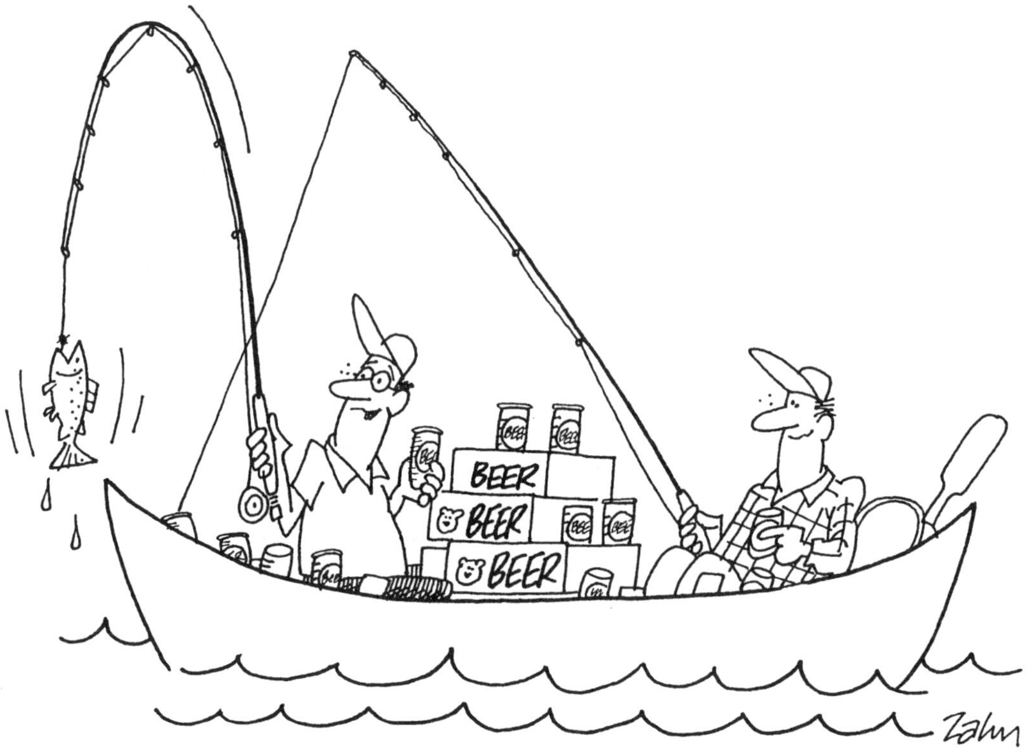
BEER
BEER
BEER
Zahn

"WELL, I'LL BE DAMNED! I CAUGHT A FISH."

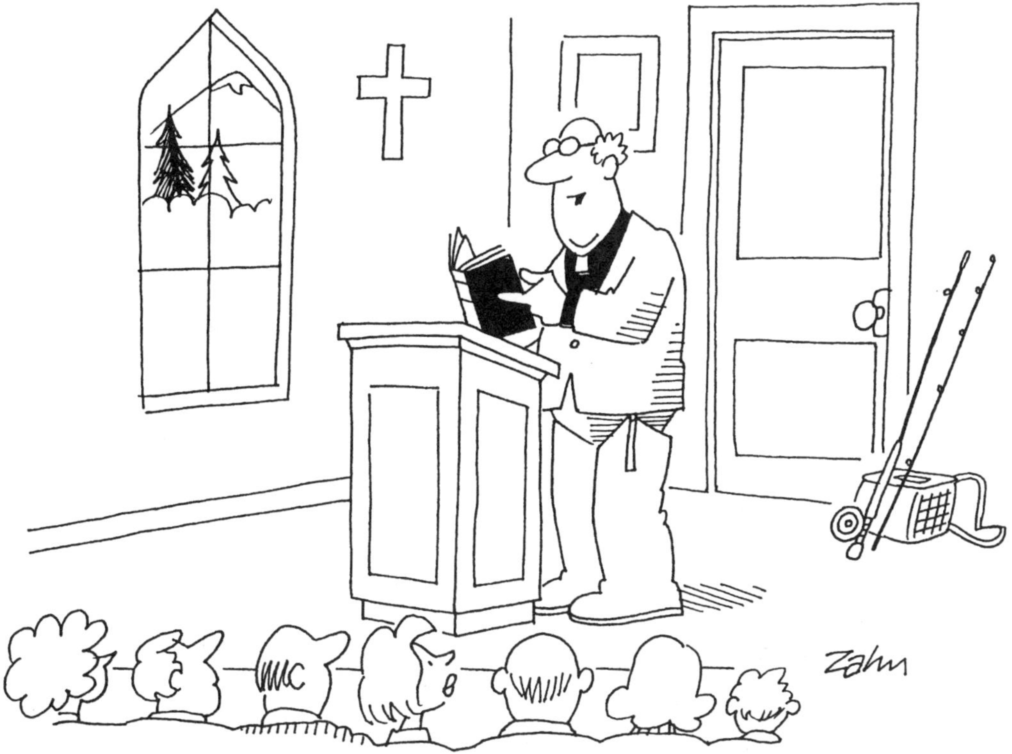
Zahn

"I'M GOING TO CUT MY SERMON SHORT THIS MORNING BECAUSE OF A DIVINE HATCH!"

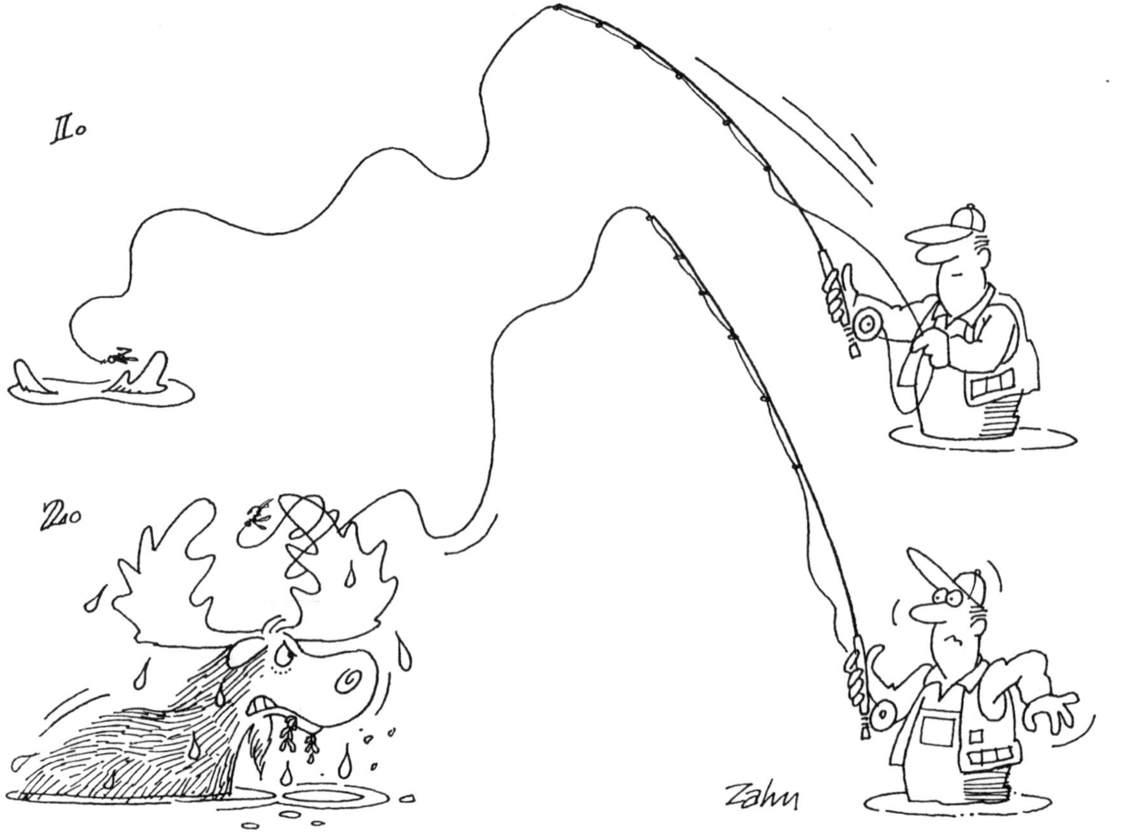
1.
2.
Zahn

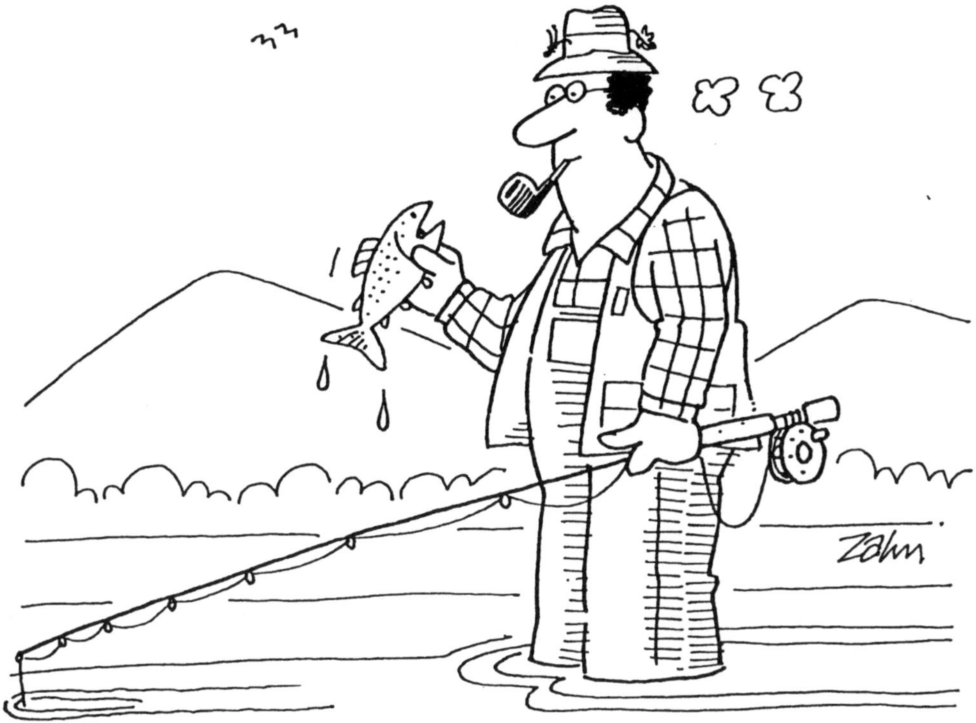
Zahn

"RELEASE ME AND I'LL SHOW YOU WHERE A NINE POUNDER HANGS OUT!"

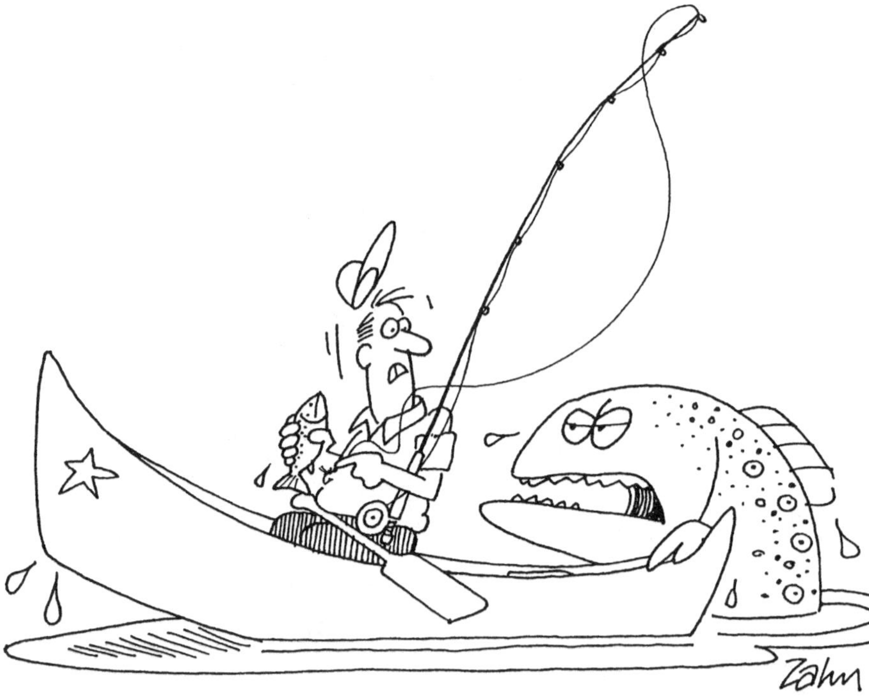
Zahn

"YOU HEARD ME.... THROW HIM BACK!"

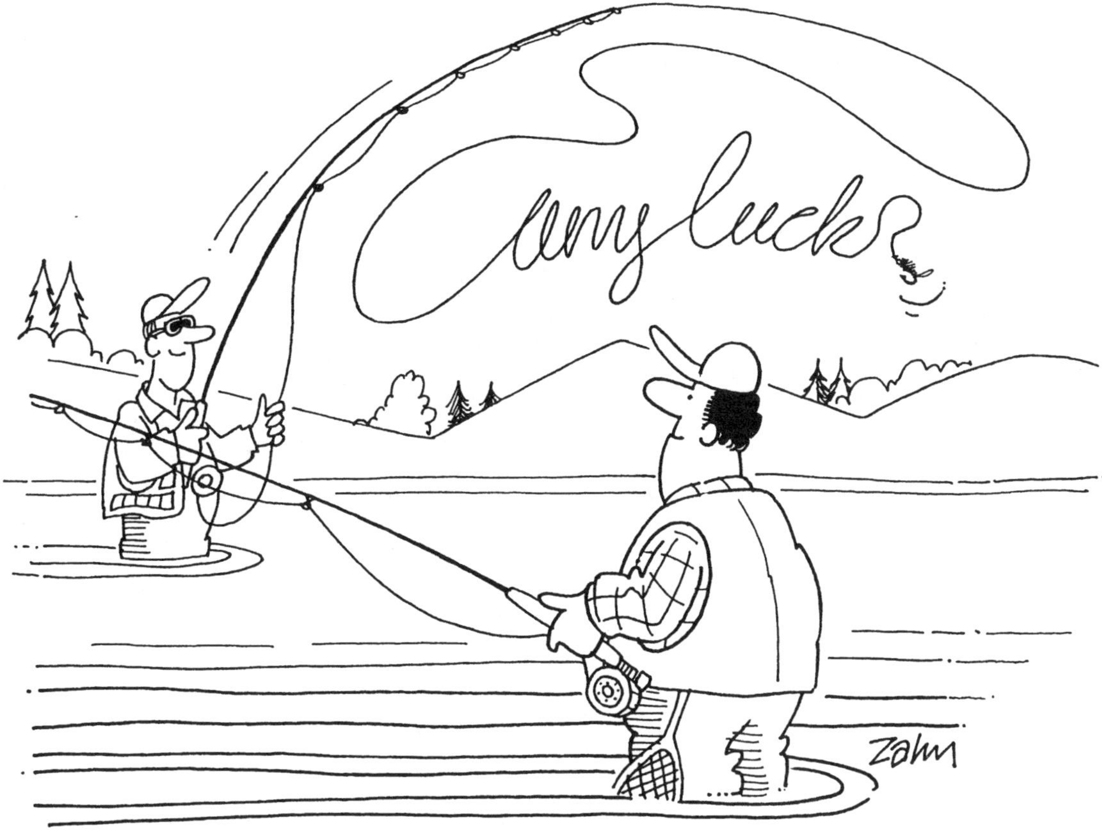
zahn

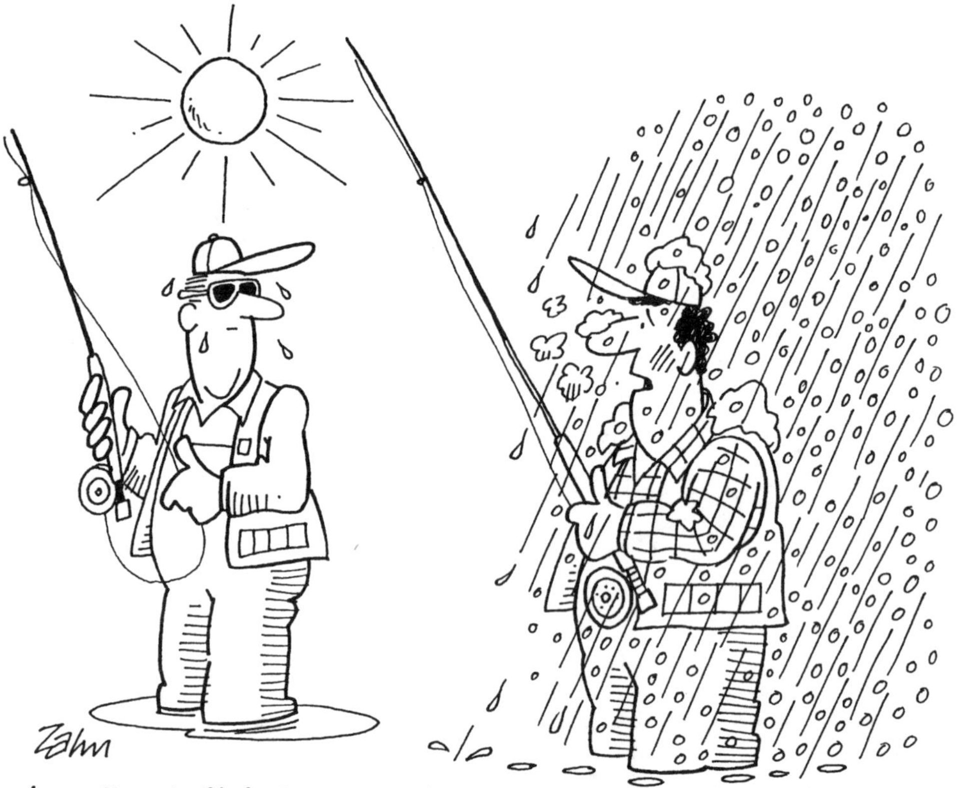
Zahn

"DO YOU THINK THIS SUDDEN WEATHER CHANGE WILL SHUT THE FISH OFF?"

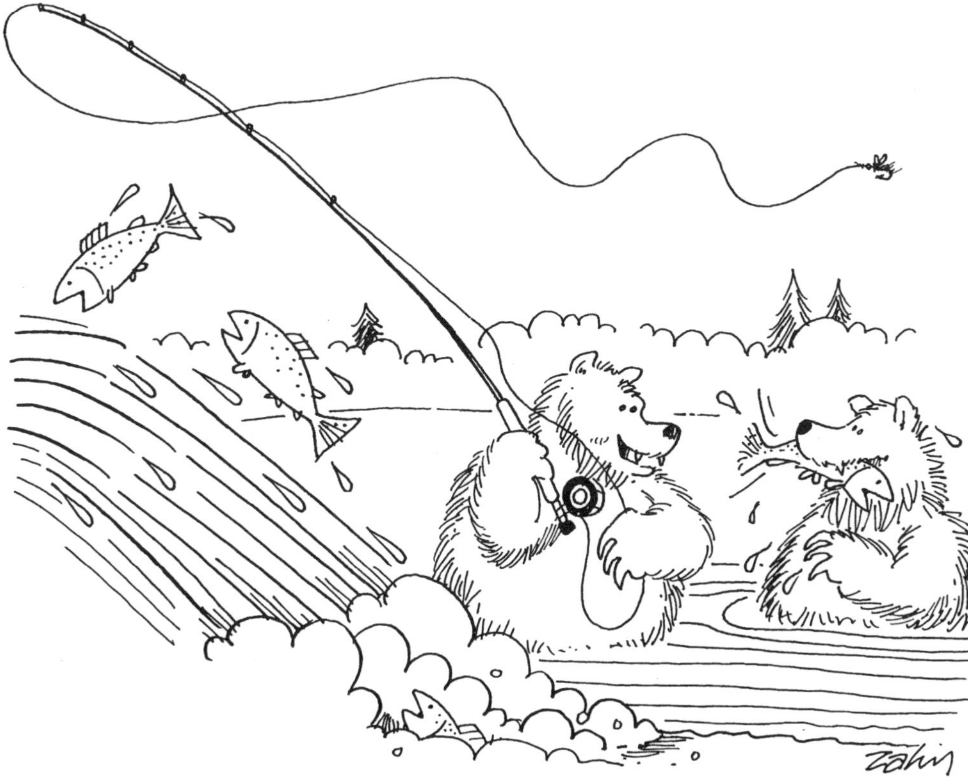
Zahn

"I LIKE TO GIVE THEM A SPORTING CHANCE."

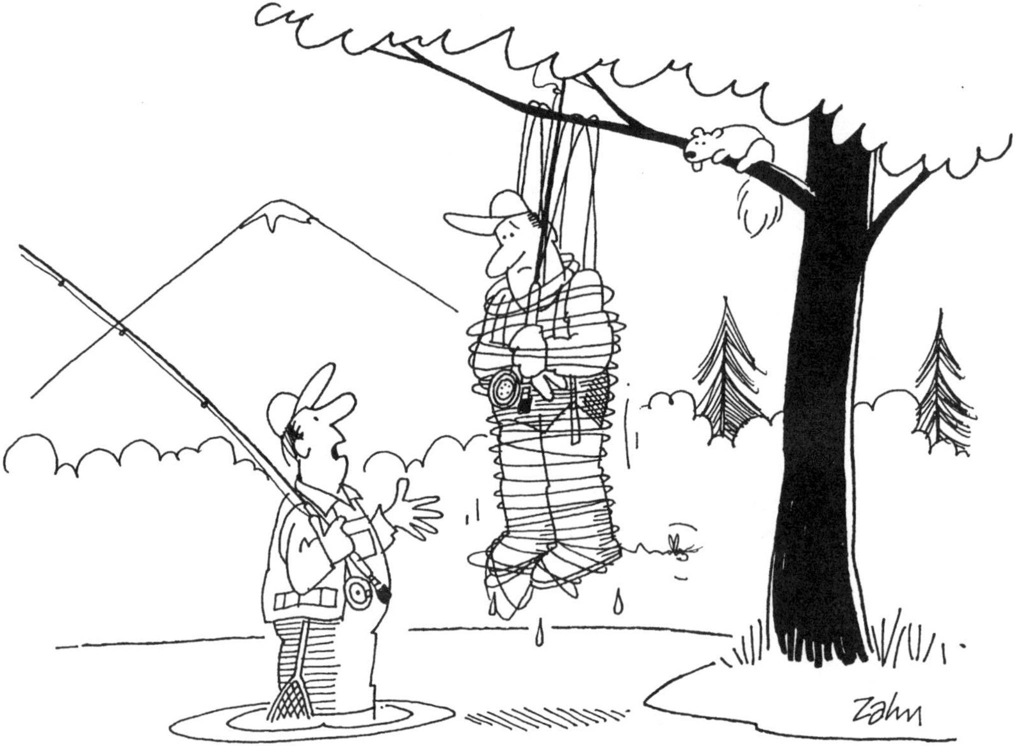
Zahn

"HOW ON EARTH DID YOU DO THAT?"

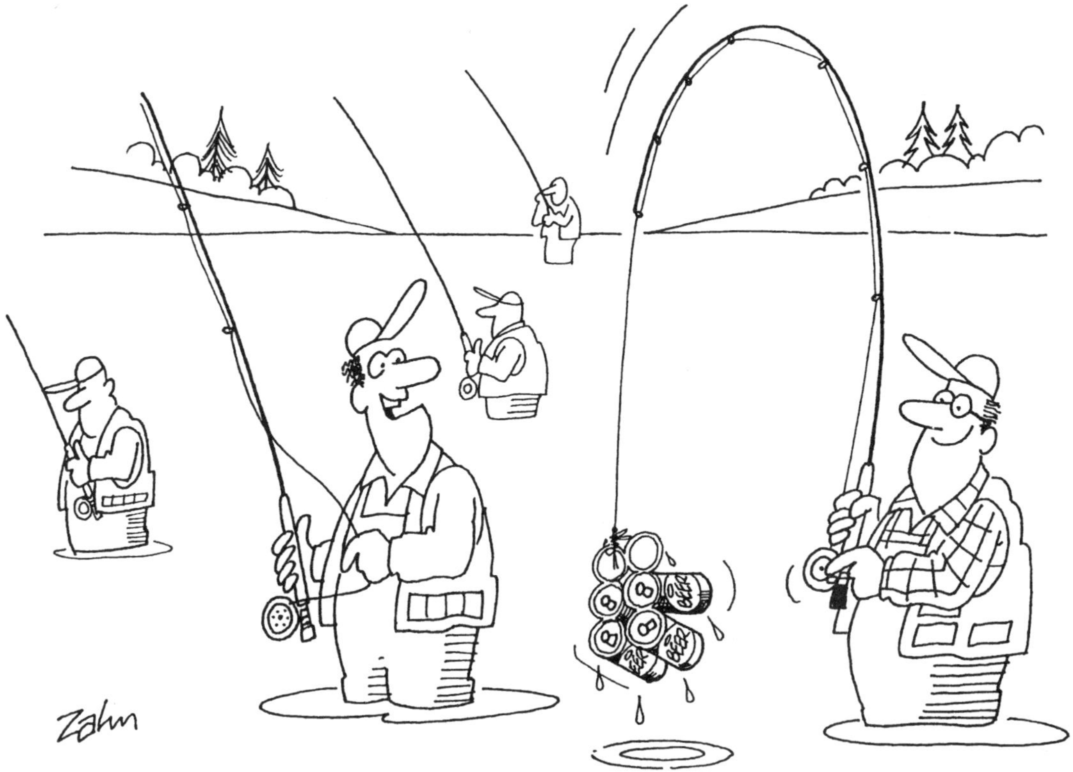
Zahn

"NICE CATCH, MARK!... THAT'S THE GOOD STUFF!"

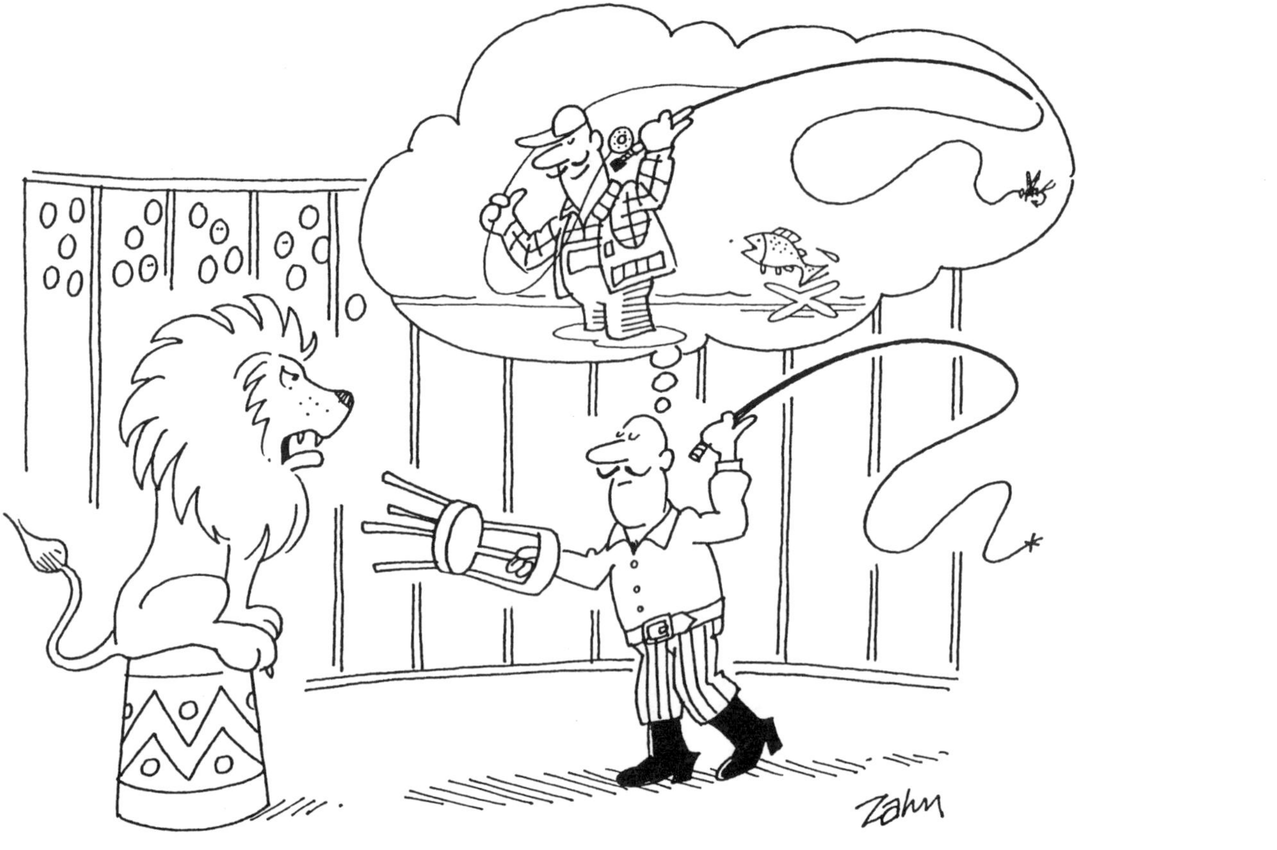
Zahn

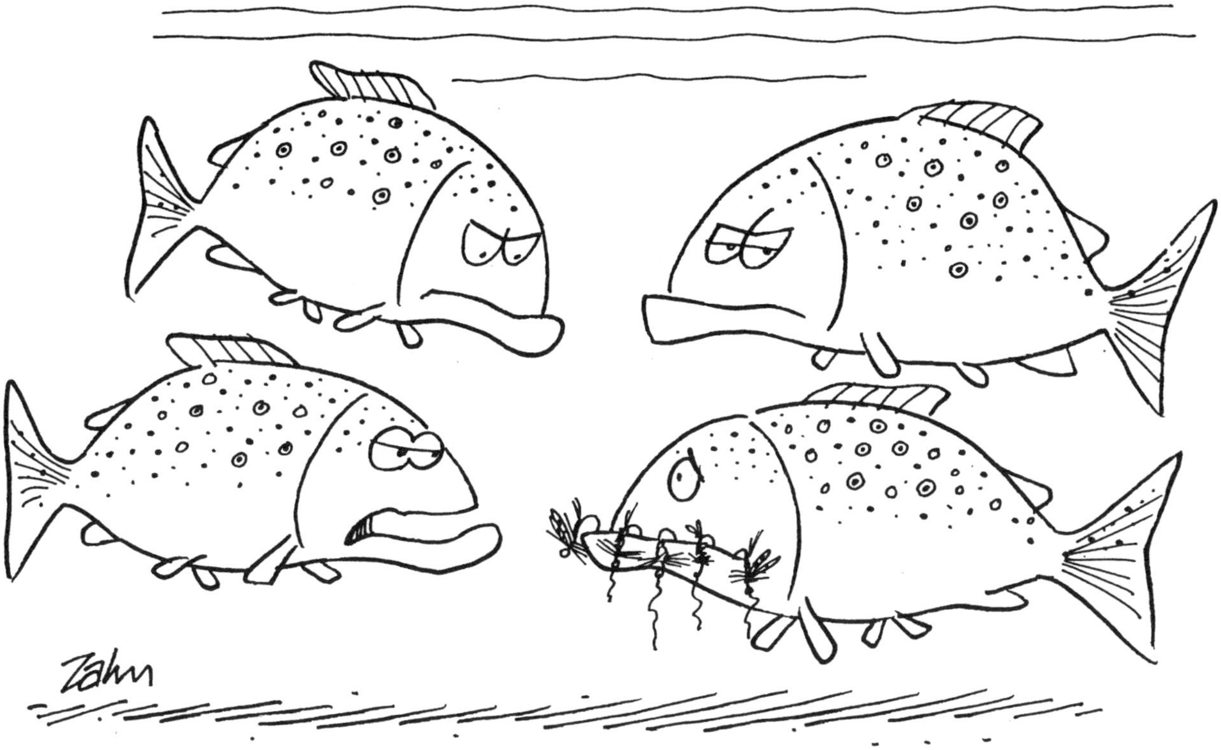
Zahn

" WE'RE SUPPOSED TO BE A VERY INTELLIGENT FISH
AND YOU'RE GIVING US A BAD NAME ! "

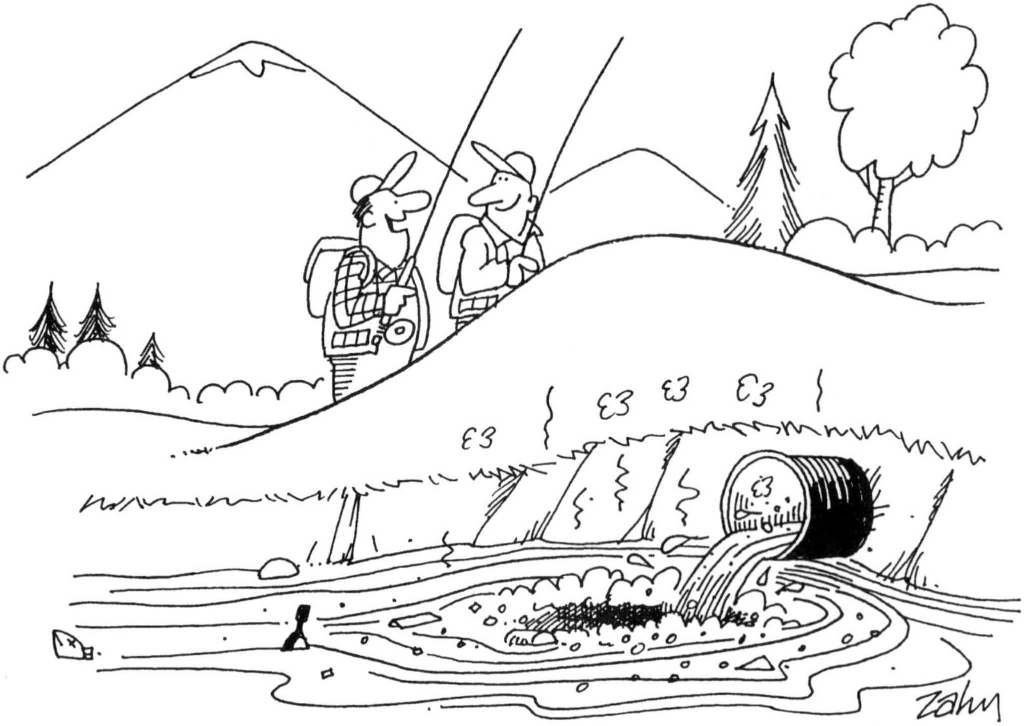
Zahn

" THAT SECRET POOL I WAS TELLING YOU ABOUT IS JUST OVER THIS HILL! I USED TO KILL THE BROOK TROUT HERE WHEN I WAS A KID! "

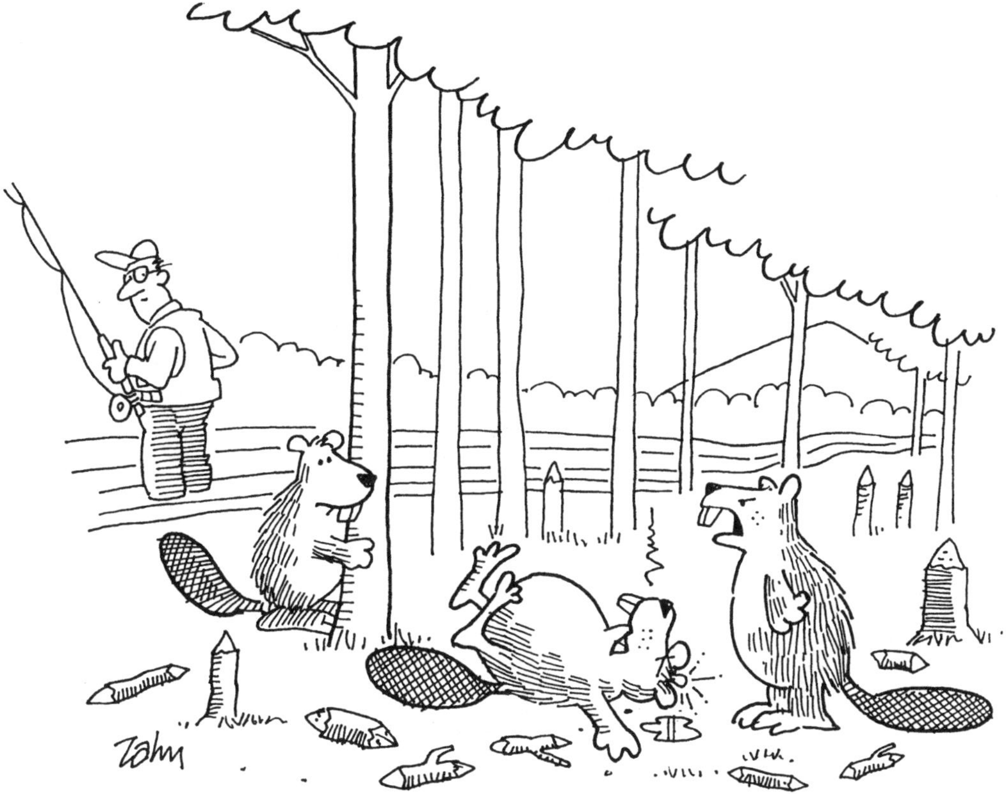
Zahn

"I TOLD YOU TWO SOMEONE WOULD GET HURT IN A FOOD FIGHT!"

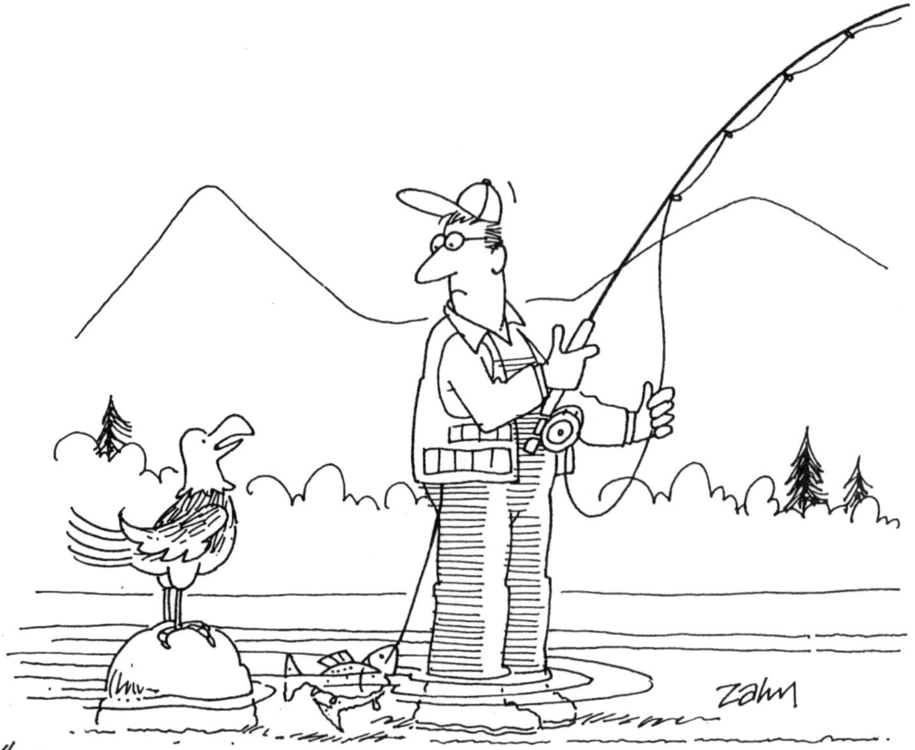
ZAHN

" COULD YOU HELP OUT AN EAGLE DOWN ON HIS LUCK ?
I HAVEN'T CAUGHT A FISH IN THREE DAYS! "

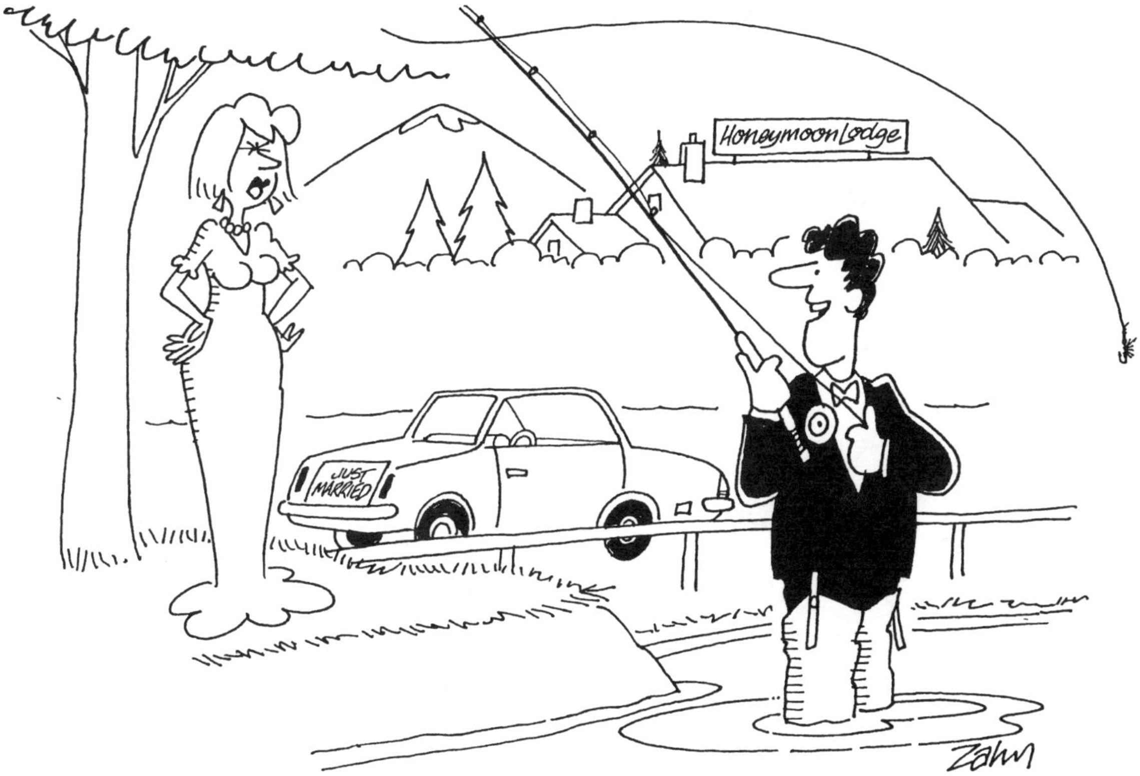

Honeymoon Lodge
JUST MARRIED
Zahn

"JUST ONE MORE CAST."

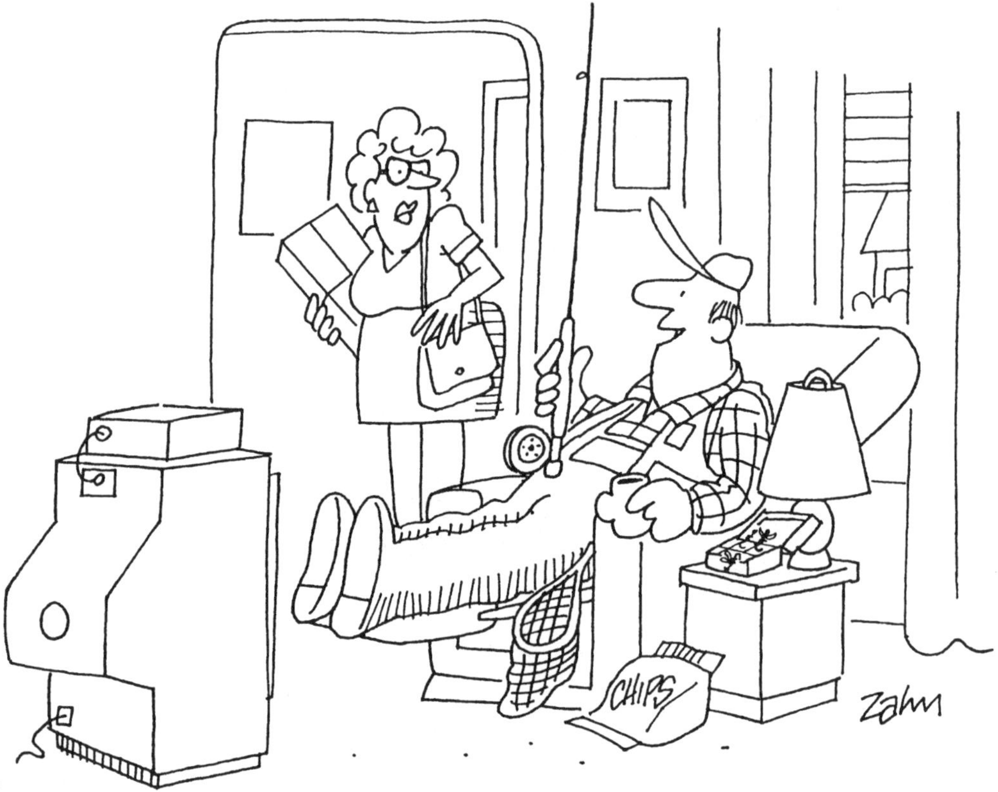
CHIPS
Zahn

"I ENJOY THE FLY-FISHING SHOW MORE IF I DRESS UP FOR IT."

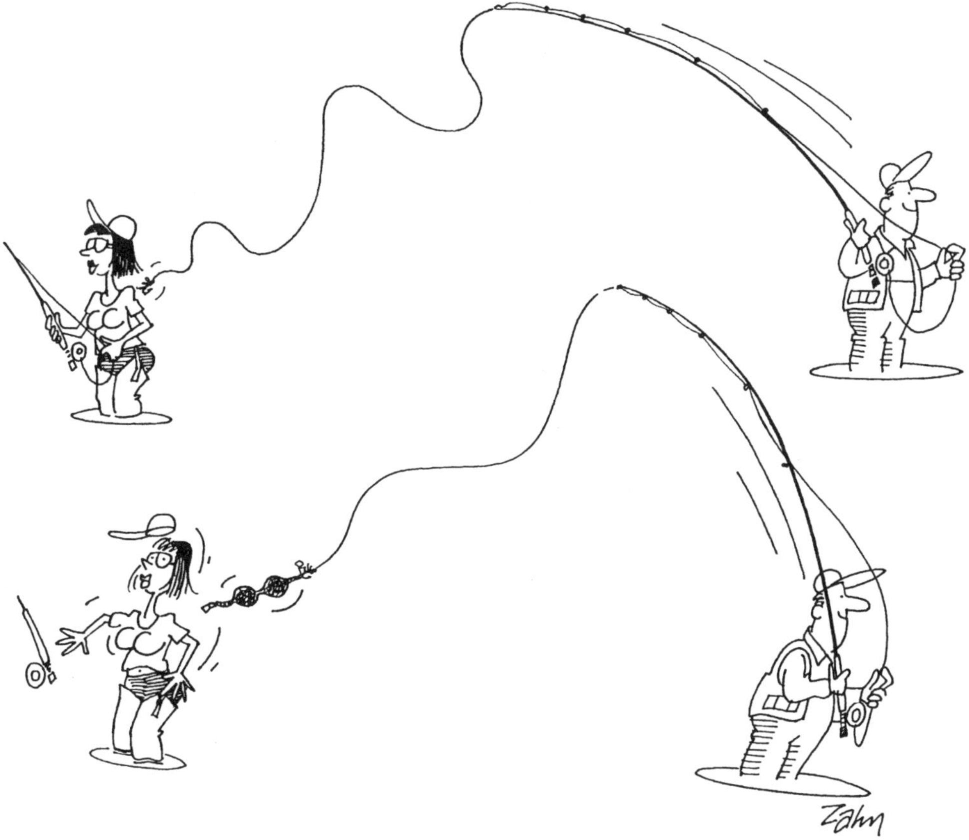
Zahn

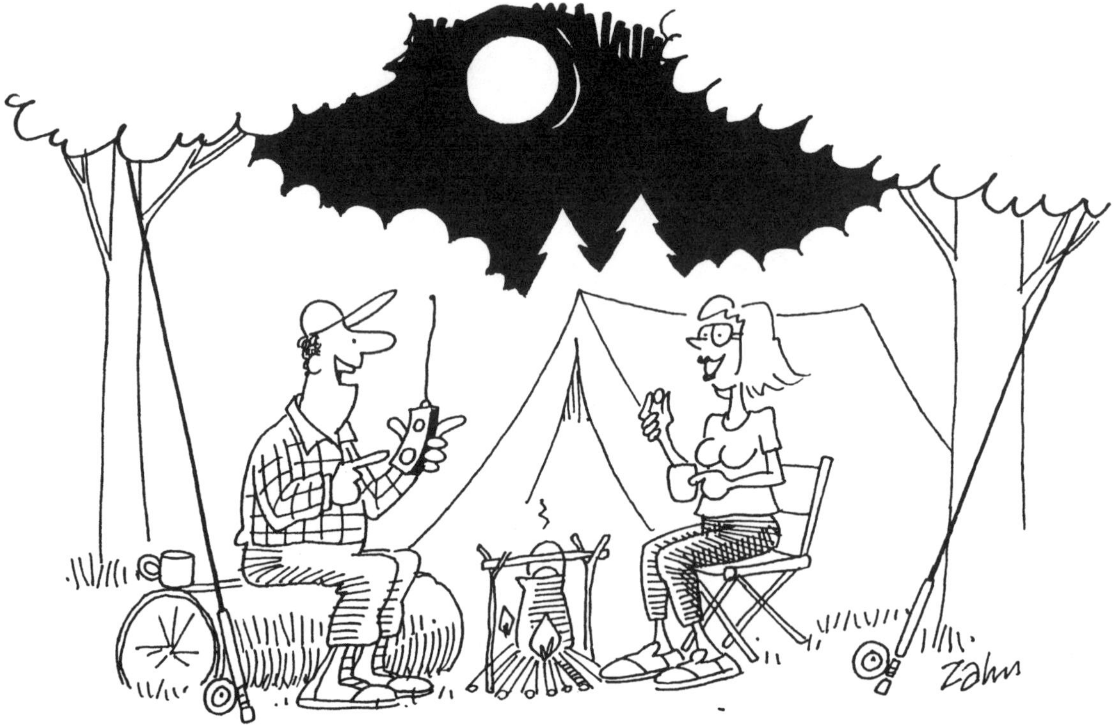
Zahn

"DIDN'T I TELL YOU WE'D BE EATING FISH TONIGHT? DOUG'S FISH FRY DELIVERS!"

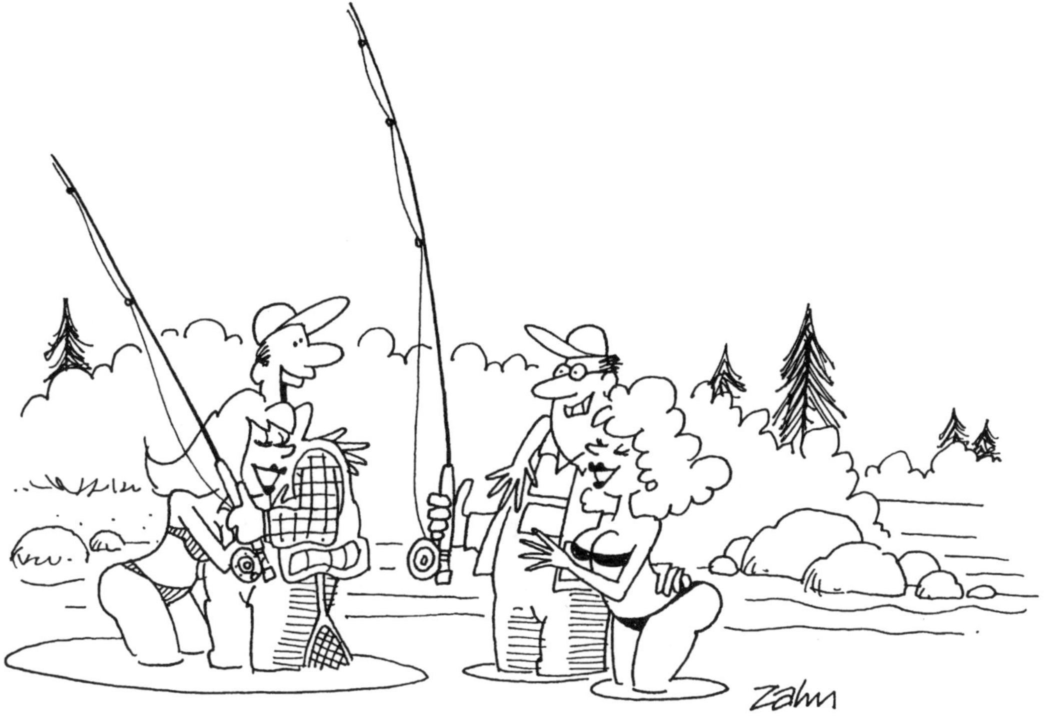
Zahn

"DON'T YOU LOVE FISHING WITH NYMPHS?"

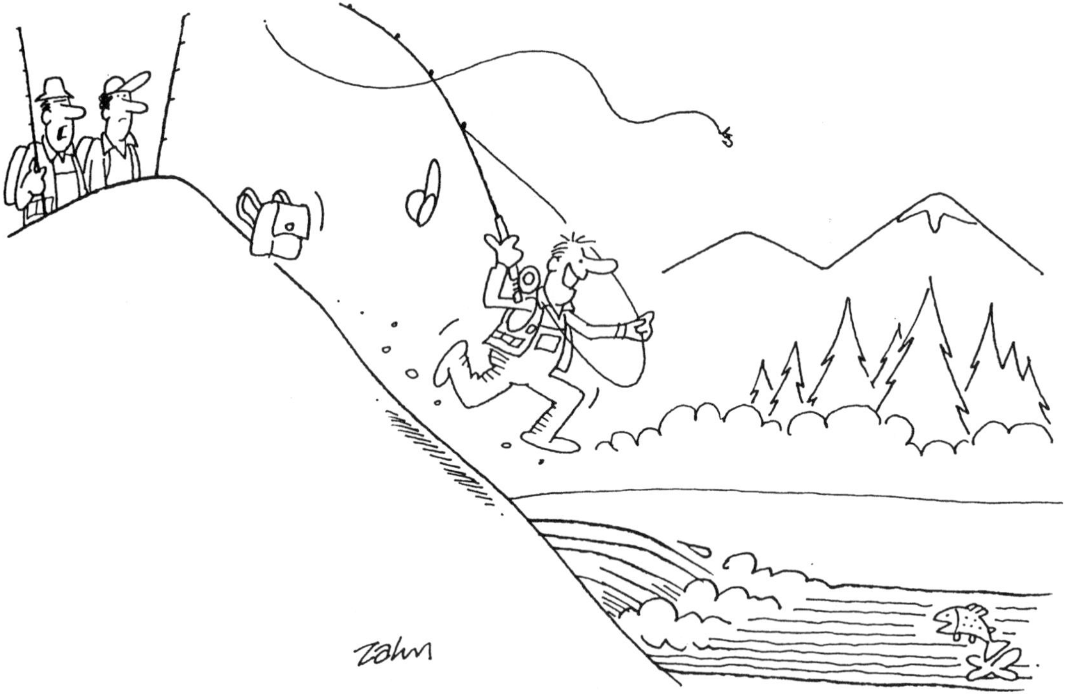
Zahn

" FRED ALWAYS HAS TO GET IN THE FIRST CAST ! "

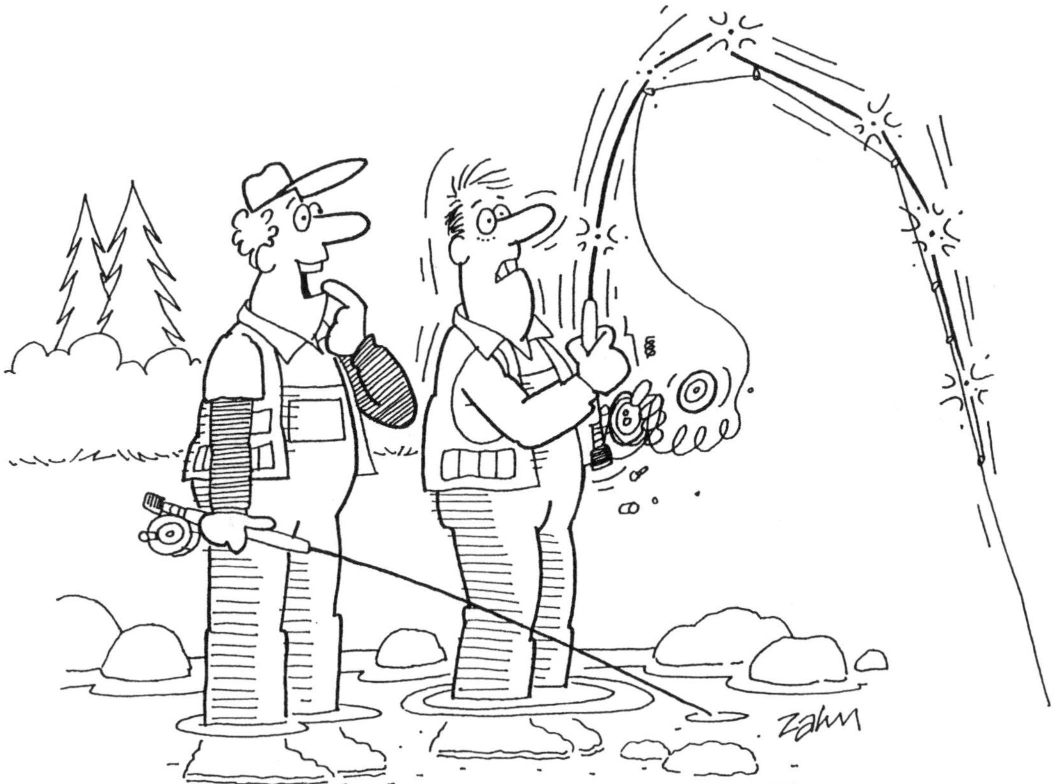
zahn

"MAN! THAT WAS SOME STRIKE!"

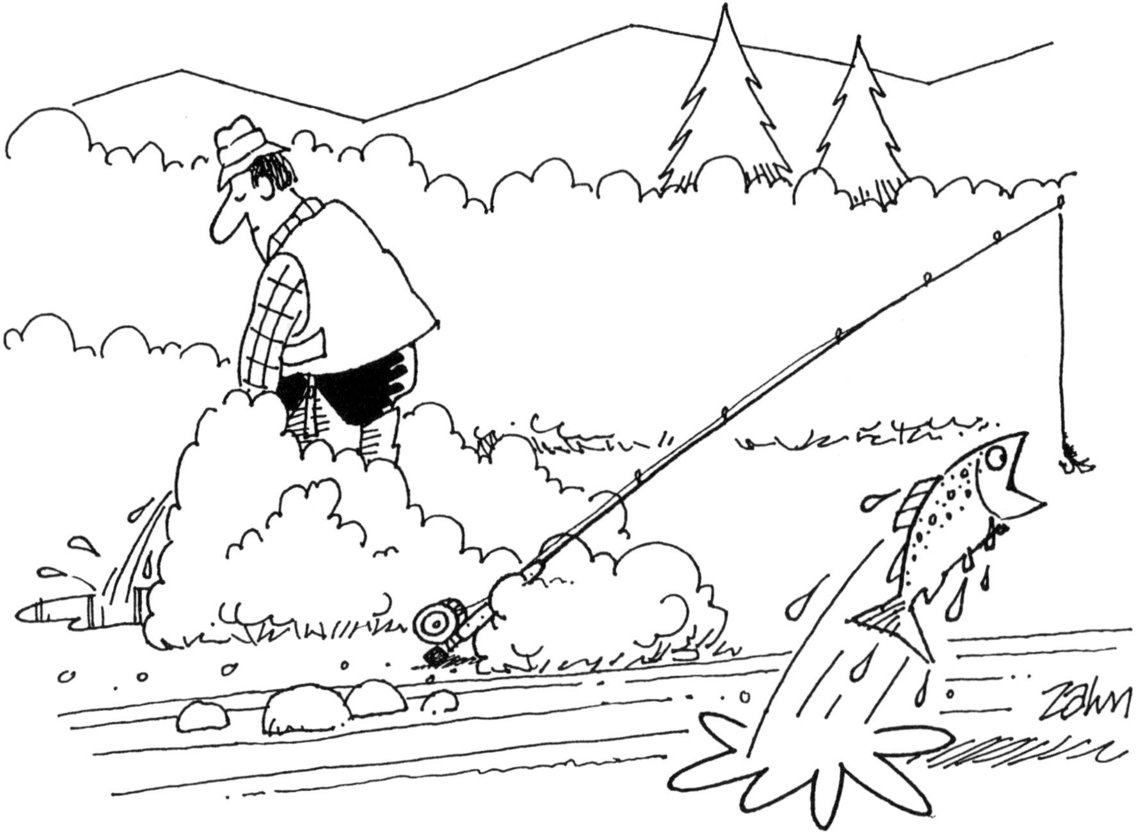
Zahn

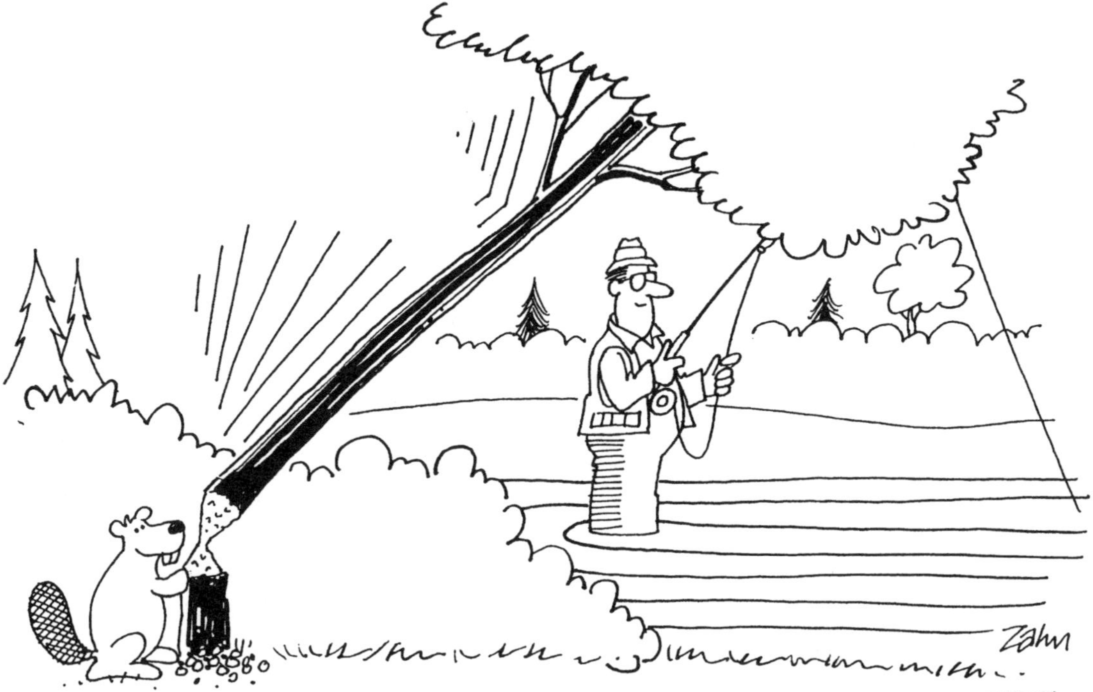
Zahn

ERWIN WAS ABOUT TO GET HIS FIRST SOLID STRIKE OF THE DAY.

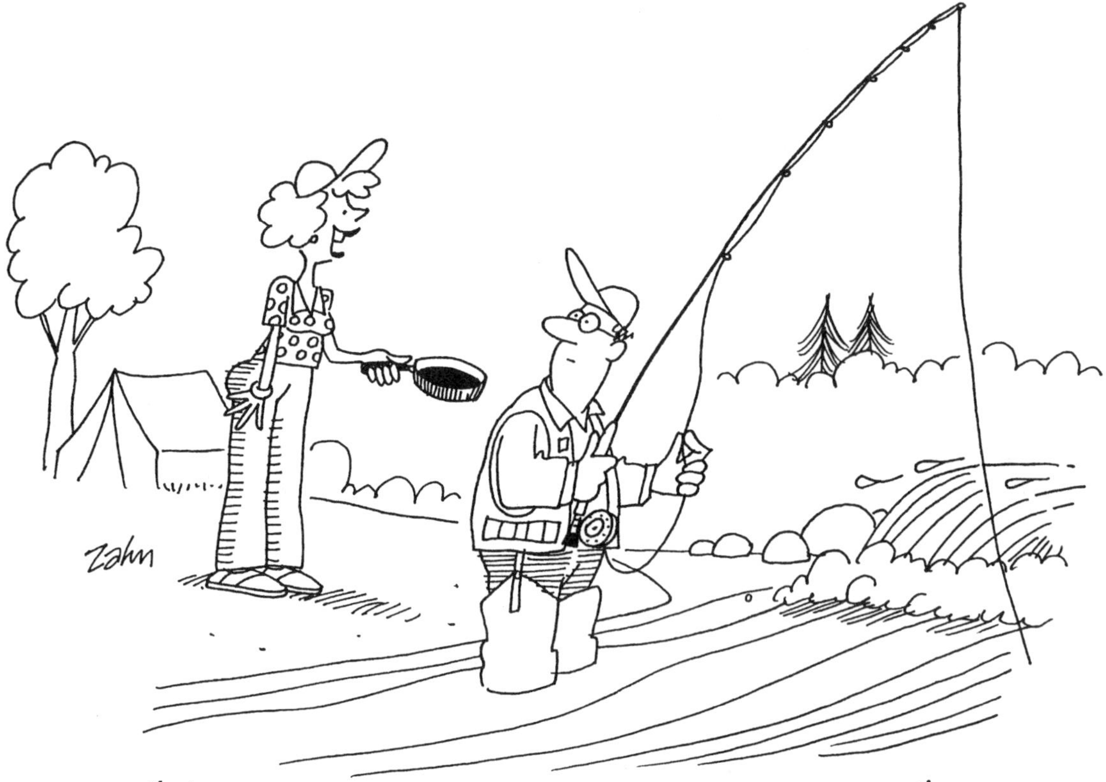
Zahn

"I'M STARTING DINNER... CATCH SOMETHING."

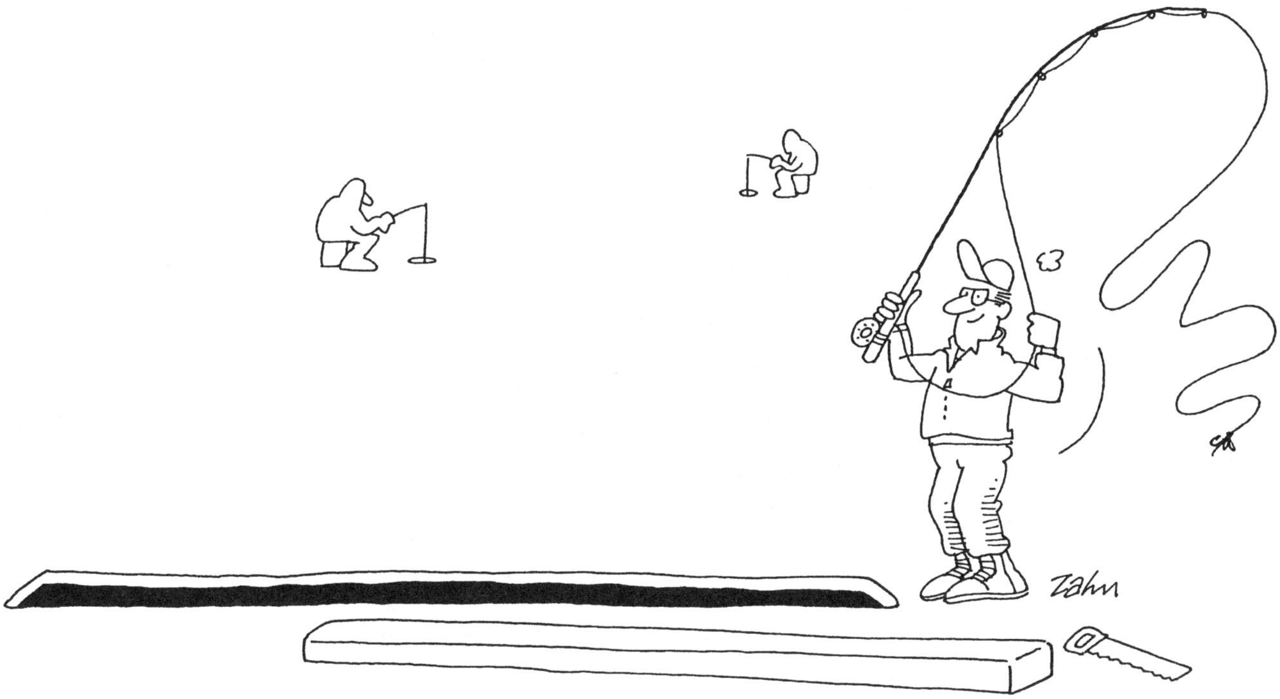
Zahn

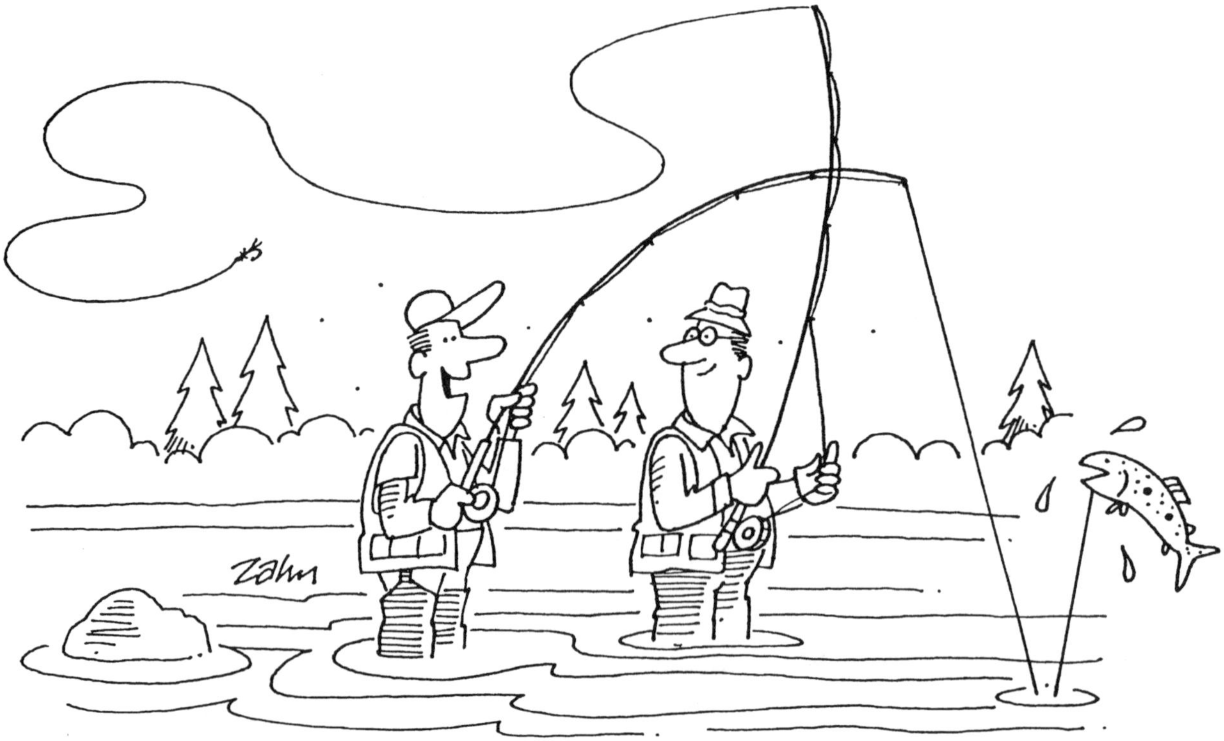
Zahn

" THANK GOD IT'S FLYDAY ! "